The cover photo is the one which Dorothy sent with her application to Southlands Training College, Battersea, London, which she attended 1918 – 20. Stuart Bremner, College Archives, Southlands College, University of Surrey Roehampton, found this in the College archives

DOROTHY

FROM

HYTHE IN KENT

by Dorothy Thomas (nee Dann)

and Ruth I Johns

Plowright Press ∎ Warwick

PLOWRIGHT PRESS
P O BOX 66
WARWICK CV34 4XE
www.plowrightpress.co.uk

**Order direct from Plowright Press £12.00 (plus £1.50 toward
postage UK), or from bookshops (High Street, independent or
Internet including www.Amazon.co.uk)**

CONTENTS

Part 3

HISTORICAL NOTE ABOUT HYTHE

Hythe has a long history. It is mentioned in the Domesday Survey as part of the manor of Saltwood. Hythe town gradually moved eastwards and settled in its present position by the time of the Norman conquest. St Leonard's Church, originally a Norman building, was extended in 1175 to provide a large nave. Visitors are often curious to see the collection of human skulls and bones in the Crypt of the Church, and to ponder differing stories of their history.

Hythe's geographical position has been a major factor in determining its history. For example, it is the oldest [1278] of the original 'Cinque Ports' – the others being Hastings, Romney, Dover and Sandwich – which were obligated to provide ships and men to protect the south-east coast from invasion before the establishment of the Royal Navy.

Hythe steadily declined until the threat of invasion from Napoleon. The Royal Military Canal and a long line of Martello Towers along the coastline were constructed for defence purposes.

In 1853, the School of Musketry was established and Dorothy's father, Robert Dann, began a long association with the School in 1879, first as Sergeant Instructor and later as Officers' Mess Steward. He and his wife raised their large family in Hythe.

Hythe experienced a huge expansion of its population with soldiers camped around it, and soldiers billeted in it, during the First World War. Many were there only for a short spell en route to battlefields on the Continent.

In World War Two, people able to leave the town were requested to do so for their own safety. The two remaining members of the Dann family left. Thus ended the family connection with the town.

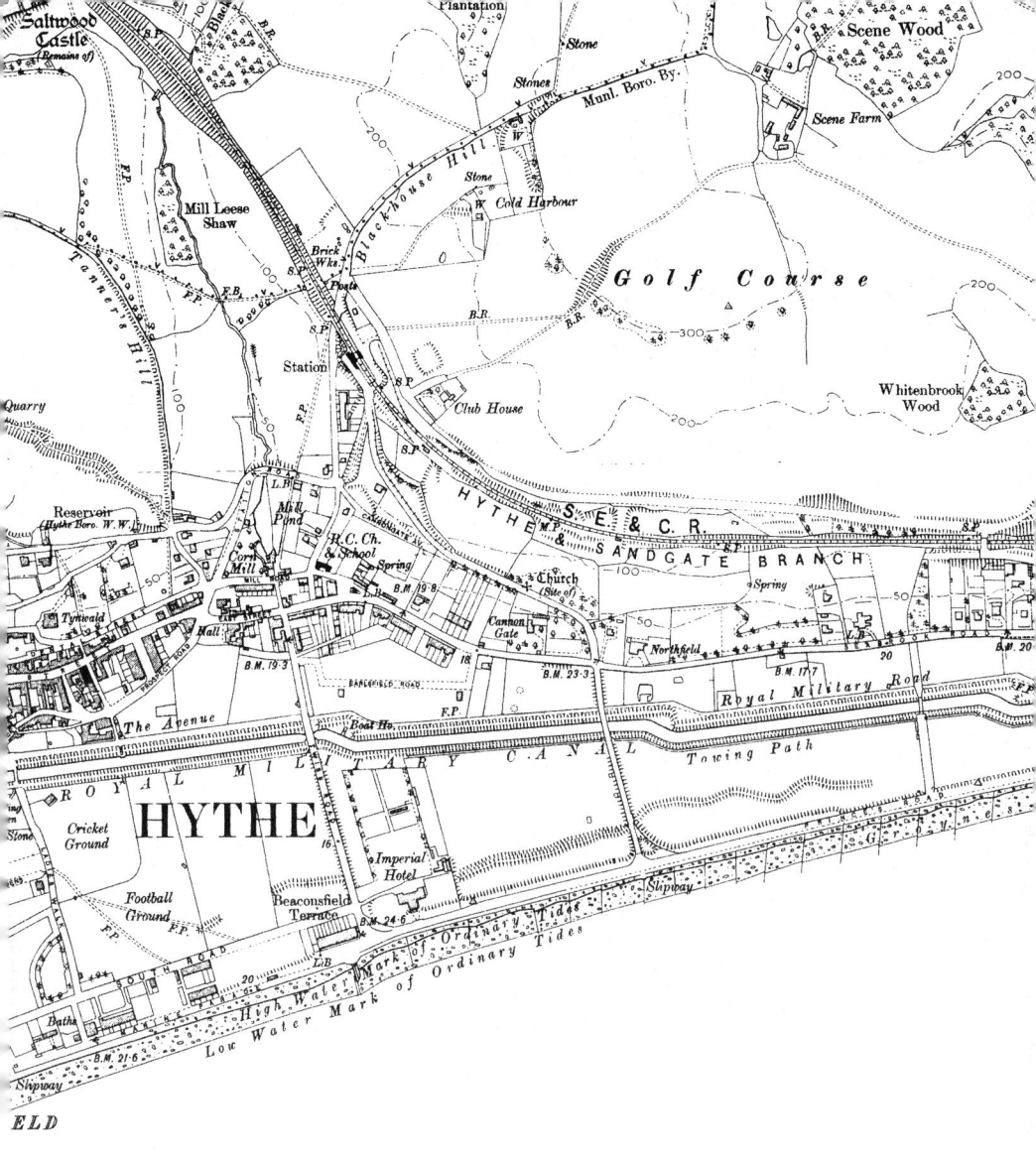

Hythe as shown on a section from the 6" O/S map 74 SE 1908. Courtesy Local Studies, Folkestone Library

INTRODUCTION

I found my mother's manuscript (printed in Part 2 of this book) among her papers after she died in 1981. She left very few worldly possessions. Her manuscript was neatly placed in a drawer of her desk in her granny flat in our home. As her sole executor, there was no doubt that she intended it for me. I cannot be sure exactly when she wrote it, but, from the context, it was the mid-1970s.

It was especially in the 1970s that she would sometimes have conversations with me around some of the themes in her MS. I believe her interest had been stimulated at this time because she returned to the classroom (as a voluntary helper) in her mid-70s. She loved it. And it was the time when she was enjoying spells of writing. She had some articles and poems published and a reminiscence broadcast on *Woman's Hour* on BBC radio.

Part 2 of this book was the most significant piece of her writing that survived. She had her own typewriter and used it much for letter writing. As she freely admitted, her handwriting was difficult to read! In her early life, she had sustained a wrist injury, which made it difficult to control a 'neat even hand' in writing, but it never affected use of her right hand in other ways.

I first sought advice about Dorothy's MS from Mrs P M Shaw, Archivist for East Kent, Kent Library at Hythe, in June 1995. She encouraged me to try to get it published, not least because there is a dearth of recorded information about Hythe life in the early decades of the 20th Century. I lodged a copy of the MS with the Library in Hythe in case I was unable to get it published, so that – in any event – it would not be lost to history.

I tried to interest several publishers. Each declined because the MS was not a 'commercial proposition'. Two said they read all the MS because it interested them and referred to Dorothy's ability to write.

In later life, I became a community historian with my own small not-for-profit publishing company, Plowright Press[1]. It gradually became a possibility that I could publish my mother's manuscript.

Dorothy's MS filled in some missing family history. For example, she had to leave teaching when she married Gilbert Thomas because of the Marriage Bar whereby married women in specified jobs were disqualified from working. I wondered how, in a family in which livings were made through communication skills, this had never seemed important enough to mention, or maybe it was mentioned but seen as insignificant. Even by the time I was a young woman, the idea of a Marriage Bar would have seemed incomprehensible unless one was a social historian (and, at that time, I was not). Nobody explained the significance of why Dorothy left teaching. Gilbert certainly did not.

In her manuscript, the freedom of her childhood and the challenge of her entry into the world of teaching that she loved are very evident. Was writing this manuscript a way of her affirming these? Of saying, yes, this was who I was? Her ability 'to reach out' remained after marriage but within a framework that was, I believe, sometimes difficult for her because of the very ordered way of life which Gilbert, her husband, assumed was essential.

I believe Dorothy's life story is one that demonstrates the talent and energy of a bright personality in the first generation of her family to have the opportunity for tertiary education. It also shows that, despite her loving family background, her education and her professional expertise as a teacher, she was unprepared for the life of a suburban Middle Class wife. However, she was multi-skilled and achieved much that will be self-evident in this book.

To place Dorothy's manuscript in context, I have gathered up her family background and what happened to her siblings in Part 1.

---

[1] www.plowrightpress.co.uk

Part 2 is her own account of her early life up until she married. I have added footnotes where, for instance, I discovered additional information of events Dorothy refers to. Part 3 is the story of Dorothy's life after she left teaching. Obviously, I can fill in more about her life before I left home, of times when she and I were together and after she was widowed and came to live with me, than I can about the times when Gilbert and she were on their own. I bring my own life story into the text only in so far as it tells us something about Dorothy. Therefore, in no sense, is this my autobiography.

Her use of language has not been modernised. Use of language is part of social history. Thus for example, writing in the 1970s about her student days, Dorothy refers to mentally defective children and not children with learning difficulties, which would now be the description.

In Part 1, there are a few discrepancies in the spelling of names and in dates because of differences that appear, for example, on baptismal certificates and Census records. I have not tried to unify differences because it is difficult, for example, at this distance to know whether Ann or Anne was the correct spelling for Ann Burwood.

THANKS

My thanks to many members of Dorothy's extended family who have helped to fill in parts of the Dann Family Tree, and offered photographs and recollections: especially my cousins Margaret Healey, Pauline Hughes and her elder son Peter Hughes, Barbara Kingston, Edna Waterfield and Colin Waterfield.

Thanks to Rob Illingworth, Team Librarian, Local Studies, Folkstone Library; Cynthia Bianchi, Library Assistant, Hythe Library; Derek King, Image Librarian, Image Resource Centre, Royal National Lifeboat Institution; Miss G Rickard, Genealogist; Dianne Yeadon,

Norfolk Heritage Centre; David Baynham, Museum Attendant, Regimental Museum of the Royal Warwickshire Regiment, Warwick; the British War Graves Commission; Emma Crocker, Curator, Photograph Archive, Imperial War Museum; Anthony Richards, Archivist, Imperial War Museum; Captain (Retd) P H Starling, Curator, Army Medical Services Museum, Aldershot; Alastair Massie, National Army Museum, London; Jen Young, Information Assistant, the British Red Cross Museum and Archives Department, London; Kate Masson, Assistant Archivist, Royal College of Nursing Archives, Edinburgh; Hilary Peck, Archivist, Warwickshire County Record Office; Barbara M Negus, Deputy Head of Administration, The Methodist Church; the Revd Derek Hancock, Superintendent Minister, The Methodist Church, Hythe (Folkstone Circuit).

Thanks too to Stuart Bremner, College Archives, Southlands College, University of Surrey Roehampton; Sarah Aitchison, Archivist, Institute of Education, London; Judith Etherton, Borough Archivist, London Borough of Barking and Dagenham; Simon Donahue, Local Studies Librarian, the London Borough of Havering Library Service; David Ainsworth, Local History Collection, Battersea Library, London; Scott Morrow of the *Barking and Dagenham Post*; Patsy Willis, Director of PR, Royal Star and Garter Home, Richmond, Surrey; Malcolm Taylor, Librarian, Cecil Sharp House, London; The Central School of Speech and Drama, London; Viv Wilson, author and publisher of *Teignmouth at War 1939 –1945*; Mrs Virginia Kettle; Maggie Defley, Secretary to Lord Cowdray's Agent; and to Alan Bott for help with graphics on pages 40/41.

Ruth I Johns
Warwick 2004

PART 1

WHO WAS DOROTHY?

by Ruth I Johns, Dorothy's daughter

with help of members of Dorothy's extended family,
especially Margaret Healey, Pauline Hughes and her
elder son Peter Hughes, Barbara Kingston,
Edna Waterfield and Colin Waterfield

1. DOROTHY'S MATERNAL BIRTH FAMILY

Charles Marriott, Dorothy's maternal great-grandfather, was a shoemaker. He married Jane who died in childbirth aged twenty-seven in 1838. In that year, Charles was also the Parish Clerk at Hatfield Broad Oak in Hertfordshire, where he and Jane baptised four children (Charles in 1832, Henry in 1834, James in 1836 and Harriett in 1838). Baby Harriett, died three months after her mother and two-year-old James died a month after his mother. Charles married again (Judith) and baptised two more children (Thomas in 1840 and Sarah Anne in 1842).

Elder son Charles, the first-born to Jane, became a shoemaker like his father.

He married Mary Ann Whitbread at West Ham Parish Church, Essex, on 4th September 1854. He was twenty-two-years old, she twenty-four. The witnesses were John and Catherine Godbehear, an unusual surname.

Mary Ann was the daughter of William and Maria Whitbread. William was a labourer. Mary Ann was baptised on 30th May 1830 at High Ongar, Essex, and her brother, William, in 1832.

Charles and Mary Ann Marriott (nee Whitbread) were Dorothy's maternal grandparents. They were living in Victoria Road, Woodford, Essex, when their daughter Martha (Dorothy's mother) was born on 20th February 1857 and a second daughter, Sarah A., two years later. In the 1861 Census, the family were at the same address and had a lodger, David Porter, a twenty-three-year-old grocer's assistant.

Charles Marriott died, aged forty-five, on 4th October 1877, and Mary Ann's 'x' mark is her signature on his death certificate. He died of pulmonary consumption. In the 1881 census, we find Mary

Ann and daughter Martha still living in Victoria Road and working as laundresses to make a living. They also had a lodger, Herbert Pace, a twenty-year-old clerk.

For the rest of her life, Mary Ann Marriott played an active role in her daughter Martha's family.

2. DOROTHY'S PATERNAL BIRTH FAMILY

The Dann family were Norfolk people. Family oral history describes this branch of the family as descended from Danes, and the genetically persistent height and looks would give credence to this. There is also the handed-down story of this side of the family having Quaker roots, but I cannot prove this, though names like Faith and Honor were often Quaker names of this period. Honor, in particular, recurred in several generations.

Dorothy's paternal great-grandfather was Edward Dann. Records at Shotesham All Saints, Norfolk, show that Edward was married twice, firstly to Maria and later to Honor who was mother of James who was baptised on 24th July 1825. At the time of the 1851 Census, Edward (53), an agricultural worker, and Honor (52) registered three children, James (25) agricultural labourer, Honor (16), Mary (12), granddaughter Susan (5) and Anne Burwood (47) unmarried former cook and sister-in-law. This Census tells us that Edward Dann was born at Fritton, Norfolk. The others registered were all born at Shotesham All Saints, Norfolk.

James Dann married Faith Gore on 21st September 1852, at Shotesham All Saints Parish Church. They are both stated as being 'of full age'. James and Faith Dann (nee Gore) were Dorothy's paternal grandparents.

Faith was the daughter of John and Frances Gore, who – like the Danns – were rooted in Norfolk. John was an agricultural labourer. Faith was baptised at West Acre, Norfolk, on 16th March 1834. In the 1851 West Acre Census, John (51) and Frances (47) have eight children recorded between the ages of twenty-three years old and nine-months. The four eldest, aged eleven-years upwards were stated to 'work in field'. Faith is not listed in this census: she was probably a live-in domestic servant. John Gore and all the children listed were born in West Acre, and Frances in East Rudham, Norfolk.

3

In the 1861 Census, James, a mill labourer, and Faith registered five children, Edward (8), William (6), Robert (4) who was to become Dorothy's father, Charles (2) and John (2 months).

By the time of the 1871 Census, James and Faith and family had moved away from Shotesham, where they had been living next door to his widowed mother Honor (65), his brother Edward (30) an agricultural labourer, and his mother's sister Ann Burwood (60) a retired servant.

Faith Dann died in Norwich on 6th July 1871. James was present at her death. Faith's death certificate states her age at death as thirty-seven, so there is a slight discrepancy with the age [38] stated on the 1871 Census (see below), which must have been taken just before she died of 'Cancerous Disease Exhaustion'.

At this point the genealogical trail took a wrong turning. I was told that James died in the Workhouse in Norwich in November 1881 with no family member present. There was indeed a man by the name of James Dann who died there at that time. Dying alone did not fit the family tradition and practice of dying with loved ones present. The address given on Faith's death certificate was St Catherine's Plain, St John de Sepulchre, Norwich. Norfolk Heritage Centre told me that St Catherine's Plain was the name of a road in the parish of St John de Sepulchre.

The 1871 Census, taken on 2nd April, for St Catherine's Plain found the correct Dann family there: James (48), labourer, born in Shotesham, Faith (38) born in West Acre, son Robert (15), a labourer born in Shotesham, as were the next two sons Charles (13), and John (10). Daughters Maria (8) and Honor (6) were born in Norwich.

Nothing could be found of widowed James Dann in the 1881 Census but records can be erratic. However, this Census does show daughter Honor S. Dann (15) at 31, Unthank Road, Heigham, Norfolk, as a general domestic servant to George T. Calver (boot manufacturer), his wife and one-year-old daughter.

4

The 1891 Census in the Norwich parish of St John de Sepulchre finds James Dann (66), widower, living in Wright's Yard with children Charles, a general labourer, and Honor, then a machinist. Susan Gore (60), a sister of James's deceased wife, was living at the same address as housekeeper.

Robert joined the Army very soon after his mother's death. But before we tell more of Robert's life story, we know that his father James, a labourer in a mustard mill, died on the 21st April 1895, aged seventy. He had been suffering from chronic hepatitis. We know that a daughter was present at his death[1] and probably also other family members. Death certificates state only the name of the person who registers the death and present at the death.

So, the above description of their birth families tells us that, by the time that Dorothy's parents Robert Dann and Martha Marriott met, they had experienced much, including family loyalty and hardship of survival. Both had started work at the earliest opportunity to assist their families. Both had experienced the death of a parent and belonged (as many did at that time) to families and communities where death of a mother in childbirth and/or of children was not uncommon.

---

[1] The name Dann appears, stated to be a daughter, with an unclear initial which is most probably 'M' i.e. Maria.

3. ROBERT DANN'S ARMY CAREER

When he was fourteen, Dorothy's father – Robert Dann – was working as a labourer. His mother Faith (nee Gore) had recently died of cancer aged thirty-seven. Robert, the middle son of five brothers with two younger sisters, decided to leave Norfolk to join the Army or maybe his father advised him to do so. It was a bold step. Robert's birth family were well rooted in Norfolk.

He joined the Army in 1872, in the 2/6 Foot [as it used to be called[1]] that became the 2nd Battalion Royal Warwickshire Regiment in 1881. Afterwards, he served in the 1st Battalion of the Coldstream Guards where, for a time, he was Drill Instructor at the renowned Guards Depot at Caterham. He joined the Hythe School of Musketry[2] in August 1879 where he served for forty-five-and-a-half years, first as a Sergeant Instructor then as Officers' Mess Steward. He spent over fifty-two years with the Army.

In the early 1880s, Robert Dann did most of the experimental shooting on the ranges, especially during the transitory period of the H M rifle and the Lee Metford. He met with a nasty accident during this time, according to a report in the *Folkstone Herald* on the occasion of his retirement in 1925. He was sighting a rifle, 'sent from Enfield', up to 2,000 yards, when something went wrong and the cartridge case was blown out of the breech end, cutting a deep

---

1 Before the renaming in 1881, there were two Warwickshire Regiments, the Sixth Foot and the Twenty-fourth Foot. Robert was in the 2nd Battalion of the Sixth Foot, thus 2/6.

2 The School of Musketry was formed at Hythe in 1853 'for the instruction in the Army in rifle and target practice'. In 1919, its name changed to the Small Arms School. The term 'Hythe Trained' denoted excellence. [From an Exhibition in Hythe Library 1995.] The Small Arms School had a close and happy relationship with the people of Hythe, and it employed many civilians. It relocated to Wiltshire in 1968. After fruitless local protest, nearly all the buildings of the Small Arms School in Hythe were demolished in the 1970s.

gash in his right cheek, destroying a number of teeth and causing other damage.

He was always a keen shot, heading the School for two years. He was best Army shot in 1885. He held the rifle with which the then Mayoress, Mrs H. Strahan, fired the first shot at the opening of Hythe Civilian Rifle Club.

When the First World War began in 1914, the School of Musketry became the Eastern Command School, and Robert Dann carried on there as Steward. Many thousands of young officers passed through and on to France. For the duration of the War he took on the duties of Honorary Secretary to the Soldiers' and Sailors' Family Association, later termed the Statutory Committee and finally the War Pensions Committee. He carried on these extra duties until the end of the War and was thanked by Queen Alexandra.

When Robert retired from stewardship of the Small Arms School[3] Officers' Mess, which he held for thirty-one years, the event was marked by a presentation to him by the Colonel Commandant, Col Alan Hunter CMG DSO MC, on behalf of subscribers of a 'very handsome' tea service and tray, together with a list of subscribers in a book. Among them General Sir Ian Hamilton, General Congreve VC, General C C Monro, General Ruggles Brise, General Hill and Colonel John Hopton.

Hythe School of Musketry 1915. A squad of officers in the foreground is receiving instruction. Courtesy Photograph Archive, Imperial War Museum. Negative Q 53553

---

[3] Formerly School of Musketry.

Dorothy always referred to her father's work as that of Steward. During her lifetime that was what he was. She knew a lot about soldiers passing through Hythe during the First World War but nothing about her father's accident when testing a gun long before she was born and never spoke of him as an instructor. That part of his career ended some years before she was born.

I am indebted to Mrs P M Shaw for finding the long and detailed *Folkstone Herald* report of Robert Dann's retirement in 1925. No mention in it, however, of his family which – as we know – was his first priority.

Robert Dann when he was Officers' Mess Steward at the School of Musketry. This photo – like a number taken of members of the Dann family from this time until the mid 1930s – was postcard quality and size. It had Post Card marked on the back with space for correspondence, address and stamp. This one, for example, was sent to his son-in-law Charles Waterfield at 56, Kent Street, Upper Gornal, Nr Dudley, Staffordshire, with the greetings: "Dear Charles, Many happy returns of your birthday. Love to you all, Pater"

4. DOROTHY'S PARENTS MARRY

Where did Robert Dann and Martha Marriott meet? We do not know, but his job at Hythe decided their future home. My cousin Edna remembers a family story that Robert saw Martha's photograph in a friend's house and declared: "That's the girl I'm going to marry." The most probable time that his path first crossed with that of Martha Marriott from Woodford was when he was posted to the Coldstream Guards Depot at Caterham (and he may have been posted within London for duty). Martha had relatives in London and she probably stayed with them on occasions. At least one of these relatives kept a shop,

Robert and Martha married at St Leonard's Parish Church, Hythe, on July 23rd 1881. At that time, as we know from the 1881 Census, Robert was a live-in Staff Sergeant working at the School of Musketry on Military Road, Hythe. Martha was living with her widowed mother, both working as laundresses. At the time of their marriage, Robert and Martha were both twenty-four.

They started married life in Army quarters. The 1887 Street Directory has Robert Dann, Sergeant Instructor, Sutherland Fort[1]. The Baptismal record for two of Robert and Martha's children, Maud Mary, 1885, and Daisy Sarah, 1887, gives Fort Sutherland as the family address.

H. FRIEDMANN   STRATFORD AND AT LEYTONSTONE

The young Martha Marriott. "That's the girl I'm going to marry"

---

[1] *One of three forts built to defend the Hythe area. For more information about Hythe's history before Dorothy was born refer to www.hythelive.co.uk*

Fort Sutherland itself was, by 1907, described as a ruin, so whether it was still in use, including for accommodation, in the1880s we do not know. But accommodation conditions may partly explain why Martha chose to return to her mother's home in Woodford for the birth of her babies during this period.

The 1891 Census shows Robert and Martha, and children Robert Charles, Maud Mary, Daisy and Emmeline living in St Leonard's Road (no number stated). From 1891 – 93 the local street directory shows them living at 3, St Leonard's Road, conveniently near to the School of Musketry and the firing ranges.

According to a street directory, R. Dann lived at Cyprus Terrace, Albert Road, from 1894 - 1899, but there is no recollection anywhere around the family of anyone ever mentioning this address. However, Baptismal Certificate addresses for twins Lily Mildred and Violet Mabel (1895) state Albert Road as their address. The Baptismal Certificates for Emmeline Honor (1889) and Arthur Gordon (1891) simply state Hythe.

The Street Directory shows the family living at Norfolk Villas, St Leonard's Road, from 1900 – 1916. This was 76, St Leonard's Road before the house was numbered. Dorothy was born in 1900. The death certificate of Robert and Martha's second son, Arthur Gordon, states that he died at Norfolk Villas in 1910.

I have not been able to trace Dorothy's Baptismal Certificate, but know from her own knowledge that she was baptised in the Methodist Church on Rampart Road: the Church that was opened in 1898 and which replaced the former Wesleyan Methodist Chapel[2].

---

2   It was estimated that in 1847 there were 10 – 15,000 military men quartered in the vicinity of Hythe, which grew to support the Army. With the growth of the population, the work and witness of the Methodists, some of them soldiers, grew. In 1845, the Hythe Wesleyan Methodist Chapel opened. But it suffered structural problems, and by 1895 the trustees decided to build new premises as soon as possible. [From *Hythe Methodist Church Centenary May 13th 1898 – May 13th 1998*].

76, St Leonard's Road was definitely the house to which the family returned after it had been requisitioned in the First World War by the Military. The Street Directory shows the family at 76, St Leonard's Road up to 1916, and the Electoral Register for the Hythe Constituency 1918 shows them back there, which accords with Dorothy's account of her young life at that time. It was the home with the vine in the greenhouse that Dorothy said a soldier tended whilst stationed there. Years later, I remembered that greenhouse and vine myself!

76, St Leonard's Road in 1995. Much modernisation has happened to the house and its environment since the Dann family lived there. Then, the road was not 'made up'. There were no buildings behind the house, only open land. The last Danns to leave the house were Martha and eldest daughter, May, in 1940. When the Danns moved into this house at the beginning of the 20th Century, it was a considerable improvement in living conditions for the family. It is remembered by my older cousins for the large attic room across the second floor

5. THE FAMILY OF ROBERT AND MARTHA

Below we see a 'tree' of Robert and Martha's children. In the remainder of Part I, each has a chapter describing something of their lives. This chapter includes Robert and Martha's deaths.

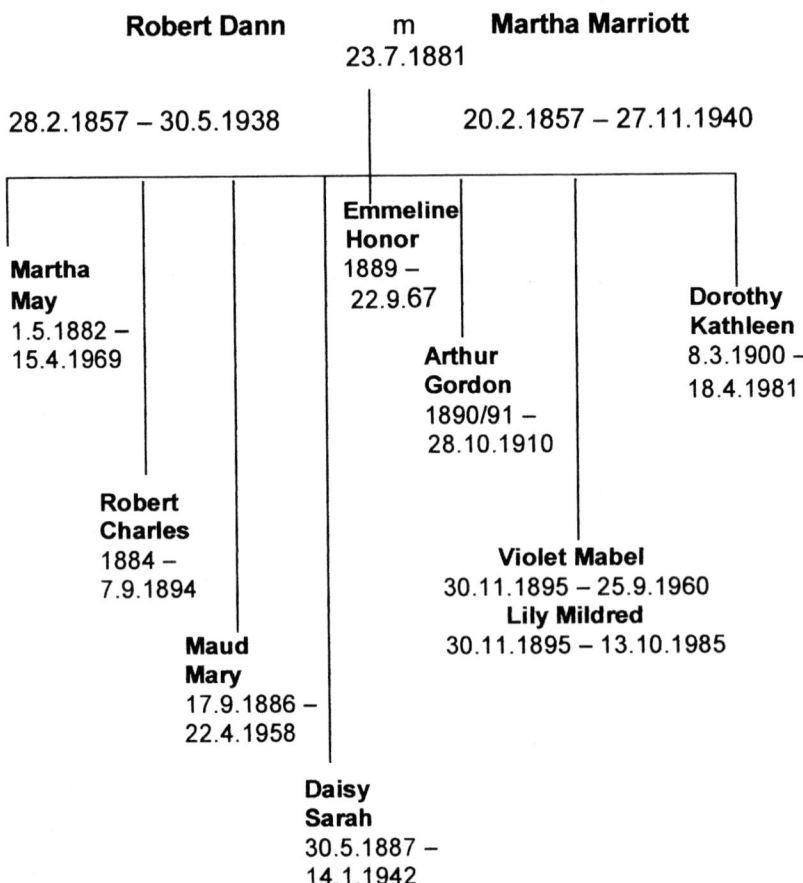

Robert Dann   m   **Martha Marriott**

23.7.1881

28.2.1857 – 30.5.1938   20.2.1857 – 27.11.1940

Martha May
1.5.1882 –
15.4.1969

Robert Charles
1884 –
7.9.1894

Maud Mary
17.9.1886 –
22.4.1958

Daisy Sarah
30.5.1887 –
14.1.1942

Emmeline Honor
1889 –
22.9.67

Arthur Gordon
1890/91 –
28.10.1910

Violet Mabel
30.11.1895 – 25.9.1960
Lily Mildred
30.11.1895 – 13.10.1985

Dorothy Kathleen
8.3.1900 –
18.4.1981

By leaving home at fifteen and taking opportunities for advancement within the Army; through commitment to the Methodist Church; through his own efforts in his own time and in

12

local life: Robert Dann became self-educated. We know Martha's mother was illiterate (albeit wise and capable). Martha could read and write and had a huge capacity to improvise and learn. I like, for example, Dorothy's story of how expert she was at cutting an egg into two equal halves and getting them cleanly into egg cups for two of her children.

Although, as we saw in the last chapter, Robert and Martha married at St Leonard's Parish Church, the Dann family had connections with Hythe Wesleyan Methodist Chapel at least from 1885, as shown by Baptismal certificates. Dorothy knew only the Wesleyan Methodist Church that replaced it and which opened in 1898. It played an important role in her life as a child and young adult. She often spoke of the Methodist Church on Rampart Road, a short walk from her home, not only as a place of worship but also for its breadth of social and educational opportunity and service. She was married there.

The Dann family is referred to in *Hythe Methodist Church Centenary May 13th 1898 – May 13th 1998*. For example: "Prominent in the Sunday School in the 1920s were the Dann family." Dorothy was a school teacher in Hythe 1920 – 25 and was part of the Dann family that helped and participated in the Sunday School and other church activities at that time, as she did in her childhood before going to College.

The Methodist Church on Rampart Road, 1995. The Church is the same building that the Danns knew from the time it was built in 1898. In earlier times it was known as the Wesleyan Methodist Church

Robert Dann in Mason's regalia and with medals. Taken in the family's garden

The Centenary publication mentioned money-raising efforts, including a book of favourite quotations printed by Lovicks in 1912 for a sale of work. "Some 200 contributors including 16 Aldermen and Councillors gave their entries. Many church members appear including Sharp, Woods, Stainer, Ellis, Chittenden, Dann, Godden, Hoskins, Worthington, Lovick and Edgar-Jackson."

Martha and Robert spent a lifelong partnership in establishing their family and nurturing their children and later their grand-children. Of their nine children, their seven daughters, born between 1882 and 1900, lived to be adults. Mindful of their own backgrounds, Martha and Robert wanted their girls to be able to 'stand on their own feet' economically if and when they needed to. This was, by no means, a widely held attitude at that time.

One daughter, Emmeline, kept her career until she retired. She did not marry and was a trained nurse. Each of the Dann daughters received sound basic schooling and, perhaps as important, a broad interactive life in her family and local community. They could all read and write fluently and manage finances. They could all earn a living.

Maud, Emmeline and Dorothy were professionally qualified: Maud and Emmeline as nurses. Dorothy was the only daughter who went on to Folkestone County School when she was twelve. Later she trained to be a teacher at Southlands College, London.

All the Dann sisters took opportunities that were available. For example, twins Lily and Violet joined the Women's Auxiliary Army Corps [WAAC] after it was formed in January 1917, offering women jobs as chauffeurs, clerks, telephonists, waitresses, cooks and instructors.

All sisters, with the possible exception of May the eldest, took some post-school course or on-the-job training and worked mainly as nurses, teachers or in clerical positions. As the youngest child, Dorothy grew up in her family when – despite the problems wrought by the First World War – it had reached a degree of financial security and opportunity which must have given her parents satisfaction that their efforts to build a secure family were succeeding.

Studio photos of Robert and Martha in their mid-70s. Taken by Charles Aldridge, Wellington Studios, Hythe

The Dann sisters who later established families of their own assumed their daughters as well as their sons would be equally well educated. This was an enlightened view not generally held until another generation following, and not always then.

We shall learn more about Martha and Robert during the course of this book.

Robert died at home at 76, St Leonard's Road, Hythe, in 1938, aged eighty-one. He died following a coronary thrombosis. Martha continued to live there. Her eldest daughter, May, had been living at Hythe and working locally at least since 1930. Other members of the family continued to visit or to stay up until the start of the Second World War.

Robert died when I was four-years old. Most of what I have learned about him has been through family members and research. He has always been spoken of with spontaneous affection, as a man of many talents, who enjoyed and cherished his family and who was content and happy to remain rooted in his local community.

My only first-hand memory of Robert Dann was of a tall man who, when I was at 76, St Leonard's Road, took me by the hand and showed me the vine growing in his small greenhouse. It is a memory of a very young child being made to feel special.

He was then elderly. I was the youngest of many cousins: his grandchildren. All experienced Robert and Martha's warmth and interest.

After she married Gilbert Thomas, Dorothy continued to visit Hythe with him. They spent holidays there with my brother, David, and myself up until the Second World War. We stayed at the Sutherland House Hotel. I remember the thrill of the Gravesend/Tilbury ferry crossing over the Thames en route to and from Hythe before our family moved to Devon.

Robert and Martha in their late 70s in their garden

The War changed a lot of things. In 1940, all who could leave Hythe were requested to do so and its population fell dramatically. Martha and May travelled by car to the home of Dorothy and Gilbert, at Leigh Bank, Ferndale Road, Teignmouth, in South Devon. It took the driver some twenty-four hours to make the journey because all signposts had been removed, pending possible German invasion, in order to make it harder for the enemy.

I remember Granny Martha in Teignmouth. By then she seemed a very elderly, somewhat fragile, woman who spent much of her time in bed because standing was difficult. But she always had a smile. She had a silver-topped cane to knock on the floor if she needed something. I still have the silver top. Our family doctor was Dr Rosalind Cooper, sister of Robert Graves the poet. She believed in chatting to her patients and that was of benefit to Granny. Dorothy and Rosalind, a forthright unconventional woman, enjoyed each other's company.

As it transpired, Teignmouth was no safer than Hythe. After France fell to the Germans, Teignmouth started to be bombed in 1940 during 'tip-and-run' raids by day.

Granny Martha died peacefully in her bed in November 1940. Dorothy was with her. The bombing had started, but she fortunately did not have to experience the worst of what was to come.

Young as I was, I felt angry that I had not been allowed to see her after she died in order to say goodbye: an instinct that has never left

6. (MARTHA) MAY DANN

Martha May was called May to avoid confusion with her mother's name, also Martha. May[1] was born on May 1st 1882 at 6, Victoria Road, Woodford, Essex, the home of her maternal grandmother, Mary Ann Marriott. Martha gave birth to several of her babies at her mother's home.

May did some of her growing up staying with her widowed maternal grandmother. May also died in Woodford, at the home of one of her nieces at 35, Churchfields, Woodford, on April 15th 1969. Her Death Certificate records that her brother-in-law, Victor Palmer, of 74, Broadmead Road, Woodford Green, was present when she died. Other relatives may well have been. Victor was married to May's sister Lily.

May did marry, someone also with the surname Dann. Her Death Certificate states she was the widow of — Dann. His first name is unknown. Cousin Edna thinks he was a Canadian. Cousin Barbara says that, in 1917, May was living with a family in Barnet looking after children. She married a man called Dann at Holy Trinity Church, Barnet, and he was from the then Empire. But he was already married. May never discussed the marriage.

Edna remembers, as a child, going to visit her maternal grandparents in Hythe when May was working at the Small Arms School [formerly the School of Musketry] and living in the Dann family home at 76, St Leonard's Road. We know from Electoral records that she lived there at least from 1930 until the Second World War.

She was still living there in 1940, when she accompanied her mother, Martha, to Dorothy and Gilbert's home in Teignmouth, which was deemed safer than Hythe at that time.

---

[1] Photos of May appear in several group photos in Part 2.

After Martha died at Teignmouth in November 1940, May stayed on with our family for a short while with a woman friend and then they left.

She occasionally came for holidays to our home in Teignmouth after the War. She could sometimes be quite critical of my mother. As a teenager, I thought maybe she was rather envious of Dorothy. I remember wondering at the difference in outlook and age, eighteen years, between these two sisters who were the eldest and youngest of their siblings.

With hindsight, it is not hard to realise that May and Dorothy grew up in quite different times. May, as the eldest child in a large family, would have had considerable responsibilities. When she was a child, educational opportunity for girls was not as developed as it became some years later. And Robert and Martha, when May was born, were setting out on their journey together and working extremely hard to create security for their family.

Cousin Edna says May was a staunch Methodist and sometimes worked as a companion, including for some years at West Byfleet when Edna lived at Walton-on-Thames. They occasionally met up.

7. ROBERT CHARLES DANN

Robert Charles was born in 1884 and died aged ten, on September 7th 1894. The cause of death was described as Acute Tuberculosis for six weeks and a 14-day Tubercular disease of the brain.

Cousin Edna found the remembrance card that was printed and it is reproduced here.

1894 was also the year that Robert Dann retired from his job as an Instructor at the School of Musketry in Hythe and became its Officers' Mess Steward. On Robert Charles' death certificate, his father is described as an Army Pensioner (he was thirty-seven and had served since he was fifteen-years old).

For Robert and Martha, the death of their second child must have been a sharp and tragic reminder of the all-too-frequent premature deaths they had both, like many other people, experienced in their birth families earlier in life.

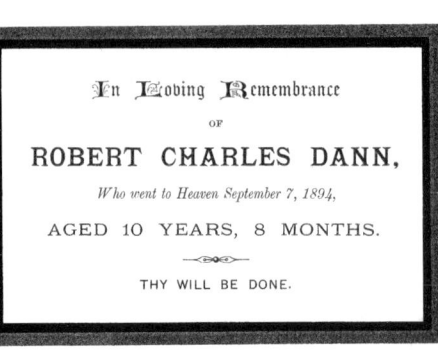

In Loving Remembrance

OF

ROBERT CHARLES DANN,

Who went to Heaven September 7, 1894,

AGED 10 YEARS, 8 MONTHS.

THY WILL BE DONE.

IN MEMORIAM

Robert's Memorial Card

The Memorial Card for Martha's mother, Mary Ann Marriott. These memorial cards had pictures of flowers on the front and small envelopes with black edging

In Loving Memory

OF

MARY ANN MARRIOTT,

Who died on the 29th September, 1910,

In her 81st year.

" Not lost, but gone before."

INTERRED AT HYTHE, KENT.

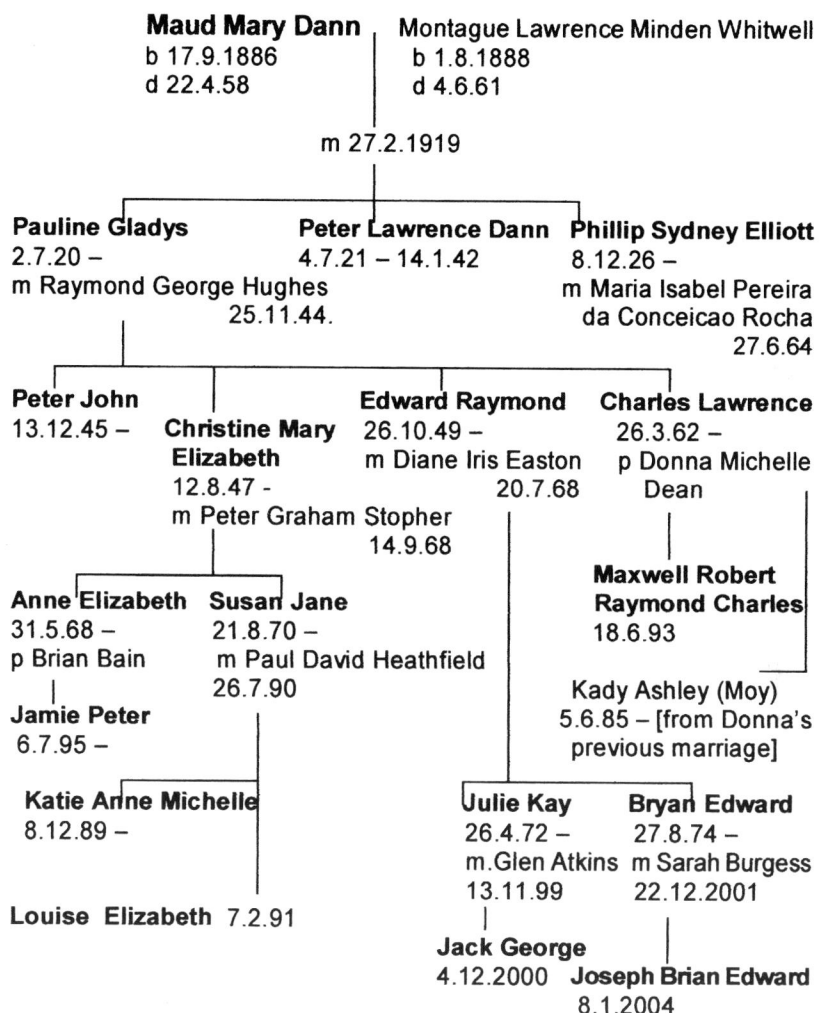

Maud Mary Dann | Montague Lawrence Minden Whitwell
b 17.9.1886 | b 1.8.1888
d 22.4.58 | d 4.6.61

m 27.2.1919

Pauline Gladys | **Peter Lawrence Dann** | **Phillip Sydney Elliott**
2.7.20 – | 4.7.21 – 14.1.42 | 8.12.26 –
m Raymond George Hughes | | m Maria Isabel Pereira
25.11.44. | | da Conceicao Rocha
| | 27.6.64

Peter John | | **Edward Raymond** | **Charles Lawrence**
13.12.45 – | **Christine Mary** | 26.10.49 – | 26.3.62 –
| **Elizabeth** | m Diane Iris Easton | p Donna Michelle
| 12.8.47 - | 20.7.68 | Dean
| m Peter Graham Stopher | |
| 14.9.68 | |

Anne Elizabeth | **Susan Jane** | | **Maxwell Robert**
31.5.68 – | 21.8.70 – | | **Raymond Charles**
p Brian Bain | m Paul David Heathfield | | 18.6.93
| 26.7.90 | |
Jamie Peter | | | Kady Ashley (Moy)
6.7.95 – | | | 5.6.85 – [from Donna's
| | | previous marriage]

Katie Anne Michelle | | **Julie Kay** | **Bryan Edward**
8.12.89 – | | 26.4.72 – | 27.8.74 –
| | m.Glen Atkins | m Sarah Burgess
| | 13.11.99 | 22.12.2001
Louise Elizabeth 7.2.91 | | **Jack George** |
| | 4.12.2000 | **Joseph Brian Edward**
| | | 8.1.2004

To me, as a child and young woman, Maud and Mont seemed an exotic couple. We occasionally met, usually in London. Mont would always kiss on both cheeks (then thought to be very French! I found it amusing).

Maud was a nursing sister and worked in France for the duration of the First World War. At the time of their marriage in 1919, they gave 35, Stade Street, Hythe, as their address. They married at the Wesleyan Methodist Church, Rampart Road, Hythe. Mont was a Staff Quartermaster Sergeant in the Royal Army Service Corps. This Stade Street address is the house to which the Dann family moved, when their home at 76, St Leonard's Road was requisitioned by the Army in the First World War. In 1920, both Maud and Mont gave the St Leonard's Road house as their address at the time of Pauline's birth. Pauline was born there.

Maud's second child, Peter, was born in Sandgate at the home of a midwife whilst the family were still living at St Leonard's Road with Maud's parents. Phillip was born at the Hertford British Hospital, Levallouis-Peret, Seine, in France. By then the family were living at 7, Rue Theophile Gautier, Neuilly-s-Seine, Seine, and Mont was secretary to H M Military Attaché in Paris.

As the Germans advanced on Paris in World War Two, he helped burn documents and left Paris as the Germans entered. Maud and son Phillip left on Whit Monday 1940, but Pauline remained with her father. Cousin Edna remembers Maud

Maud's passport photo issued in 1930. Her passport states she is a trained Hospital Sister, 5' 7" tall with hazel eyes and brown hair

returning from Paris with Phillip, whilst Mont stayed on at the Embassy for as long as possible.

When it was time to leave in June 1940, Mont and Pauline – and their pet dog 'Miss' – were driven to Bordeaux, where they boarded a P & O frozen meat ship destined for Milford Haven. However, the voyage took eleven days, in order to avoid submarines and air raids.

Peter, sadly, was one of the twenty-four thousand of the Merchant Navy and Fishing Fleets who lost their lives at sea in World War Two and who have no grave. He was a 20-year-old apprentice on the SS Empire Surf (Sunderland) when, on January 14th 1942, his ship went down. Names are commemorated on the Tower Hill Memorial that stands on the south side of the garden of Trinity Square, London, close to the Tower of London. Peter Lawrence Dann Whitwell is named on Panel 46. The Memorial is in the perpetual care of the Commonwealth War Graves Commission.

In Memory of

Apprentice PETER LAWRENCE DANN WHITWELL

S.S. Empire Surf (Sunderland), Merchant Navy
who died aged 20 on Wednesday, 14th January 1942.

Remembered with honour
TOWER HILL MEMORIAL, London, United Kingdom.

THEIR NAME LIVETH
FOR EVERMORE

In the perpetual care of
the Commonwealth War Graves Commission

Maud's son, Peter. This photo was taken in Montreal

Internet notice of Commonwealth War Graves Commission's memorial to Peter

The above is the information from the Commonwealth War Graves Commission. However, Pauline's elder son, Peter, told me that his Uncle Peter had been a Cadet on the SS Empire Surf (Sunderland). His ship left Liverpool for America but, having had to leave its convoy, it was torpedoed at dusk on January 29/30th 1942. On the commemorative Panel 46 mentioned above, only his initials P.L.D.Whitwell are engraved.

Cousin Edna has a small watercolour of The Dome of the Rock in Jerusalem painted by Peter in August 1935, so he was thirteen at the time and showed considerable talent. He gave it to Edna's father, Charles Waterfield, who used to buy Peter ice-creams when Charles and Violet's family spent holidays in Hythe.

Cousin Barbara remembers that when she was about eight (1924), her parents left her brother Brian with his grandparents at 76, St Leonard's Road, Hythe, whilst she and her parents visited Maud and Mont in France, where he worked for the British Embassy in Paris. I have often wondered how everyone fitted into the St Leonard's Road home. Phillip married a Portugese wife and lives in Portugal. Pauline lives in Enfield.

Mont, Maud's husband, in 1944 prior to promotion to Major

Pauline, Maud's daughter, and Raymond 24.2.1949

Pauline (left) with her baby Edward, me with cousin Barbara's baby Judith, and Raymond (Pauline's husband). Plus Barbara's and Pauline's other children at the time. In Barbara's garden, Barnet 1950

Photo taken at Greatstones, Kent, c1954. Left to right at back: Pauline, her mother Maud, and mother-in-law Lilian. Pauline's children Christine and Peter in front

Maud's younger son, Phillip c1961

9. DAISY SARAH DANN

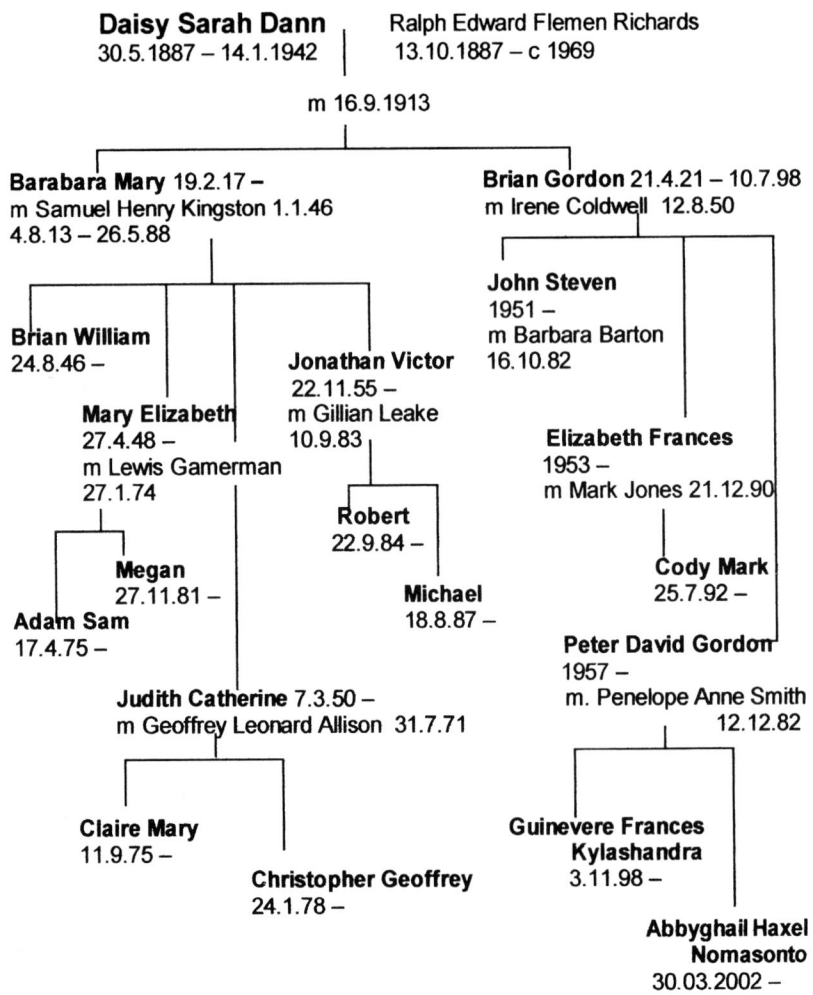

Daisy Sarah Dann
30.5.1887 – 14.1.1942

Ralph Edward Flemen Richards
13.10.1887 – c 1969

m 16.9.1913

Barabara Mary 19.2.17 –
m Samuel Henry Kingston 1.1.46
4.8.13 – 26.5.88

Brian Gordon 21.4.21 – 10.7.98
m Irene Coldwell 12.8.50

Brian William
24.8.46 –

Mary Elizabeth
27.4.48 –
m Lewis Gamerman
27.1.74

Jonathan Victor
22.11.55 –
m Gillian Leake
10.9.83

John Steven
1951 –
m Barbara Barton
16.10.82

Elizabeth Frances
1953 –
m Mark Jones 21.12.90

Megan
27.11.81 –

Adam Sam
17.4.75 –

Robert
22.9.84 –

Michael
18.8.87 –

Cody Mark
25.7.92 –

Judith Catherine 7.3.50 –
m Geoffrey Leonard Allison 31.7.71

Peter David Gordon
1957 –
m. Penelope Anne Smith
12.12.82

Claire Mary
11.9.75 –

Christopher Geoffrey
24.1.78 –

**Guinevere Frances
Kylashandra**
3.11.98 –

**Abbyghail Haxel
Nomasonto**
30.03.2002 –

Daisy was an un-certificated teacher at Hythe before she married. After the birth of her second child, she suffered bad health. Dorothy believed this was due to the afterbirth not being properly expelled. The midwife did not dare to tell the doctor because of medical

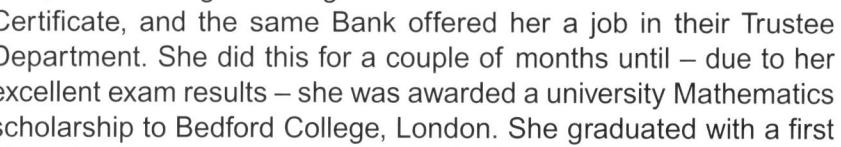

Dorothy and her mother, Martha, with Daisy's children Barbara (with Kent College, Folkestone, hatband) and Brian, mid-1920s

protocol at that time. Barbara was about eight-years old when her mother had a hysterectomy, and later she suffered breast cancer.

Daisy's husband, Ralph, was a Bank Clerk when a Bank Inspector found he was embezzling money. Previously, Ralph had borrowed money from friends and relatives. He lost his job but was not imprisoned. Barbara, at the time, was taking her Higher School Certificate, and the same Bank offered her a job in their Trustee Department. She did this for a couple of months until – due to her excellent exam results – she was awarded a university Mathematics scholarship to Bedford College, London. She graduated with a first class degree.

Her brother, Brian, was also offered a job in the same Bank. But, he joined the Royal Navy in the Second World War, working first on an escort ship for trans-Atlantic convoys and then on submarines. When given the opportunity, he opted for

Daisy when she was living at Bexhill. Barbara says this studio photo of her mother was taken, together with one of her father, and put in a folding frame for her when she left home to go to College

submarines because of the camaraderie on board. He first met his wife-to-be, Irene, at Scapa Flow Naval base. She and her sister had jobs there.

After the War, companies sought officers for employment. Brian joined a Tea Company and for many years he was a Tea Planter in Ceylon. Barbara sometimes helped his and Irene's children in school holidays. After the British left Ceylon, Brian trained for the Church of England Ministry and became a Vicar in Hampshire. Barbara and Irene are still regularly in touch.

After graduating, Barbara did a Teachers' Training Course in Cambridge for a year and then taught Mathematics in Secondary Schools, first in Southport for four years and then in Ware for four years. Later, she returned to teaching and also marked public examination Mathematics papers well into her retirement years.

Daisy and Ralph ran a Boarding House in Bexhill after he left the Bank. Wartime air raids and lack of holidaymakers ended that business, and Ralph took a job with the Army. He started embezzling again and was prosecuted and sent to prison. Barbara was able to get a 'nice little flat' in Southport, where her mother joined her and she was able to care for Daisy until her death in 1942.

Barbara then moved to Ware. She had nowhere to live. Her Head Teacher suggested she contact the local Curate's wife who wanted to share the house because her husband was being Called Up for Army Service. The Curate's brother, Sam, was a Japanese Prisoner of War. When he eventually came home, he and Barbara met and married. He later became a Bank Manager and their family of four were raised in Barnet, Hertfordshire, in a house where Barbara still lives.

Ralph did 'surface' again, some years after his children were married and had families. He had a second wife and young baby. This wife left him. Brian helped his father in his high age.

Barbara's talent for Mathematics has continued down the generations. For example, one of Barbara's grandsons teaches Mathematics in a school, in which he is the only White person, in the United States.

From my mid-teens until after my marriage at twenty-two, I spent a week, and sometimes two, in Barnet with Barbara every summer and enjoyed being with her and her family. Sometimes cousin Pauline would drop in with hers. Barbara always coped with efficiency and humour. Her home was welcoming and Barbara was never pre-occupied with impressing anybody with the latest furnishings or fashions. Until well over eighty, Barbara ran a brilliant allotment. She was what would now be called a 'role model' for me! She was seventeen years younger than my mother, Dorothy, and I am seventeen years younger than Barbara.

Daisy's daughter Barbara with three of her children and a neighbour's child taking over my 1939 car! Cars were not so easy to dent then! I had driven up to Barnet from Exeter where I was working. Summer 1954

When growing up, Barbara says – of the wider extended family – that she knew only two great-aunts, Honor and Mercy, and a cousin, Faith.

After Dorothy died, cousin Barbara wrote: ". . . My thoughts of my Aunty Dorothy go back about sixty years when I would listen enthralled to tales of children she taught – before I went to school myself. Later, there were holidays at Gidea Park and Teignmouth with vivid recollections of her kindness and humour . . . I phoned Margaret and left her to break the news to Lily who will I fear be much distressed, particularly as she is now the only representative of her generation."

Barbara and Dorothy, Hythe beach c1920

Emmeline was born in 1889. She was the sister Dorothy saw most often throughout her married life. Because Emmeline remained in nursing, living in, and – without a family or her own home – it was comfortable for her to spend her holidays with our family for several weeks each year.

In the Royal College of Nursing Archives, Emmeline appears in the RCN's printed Register of Nurses 1916-23 as a member. She trained at the Royal Berkshire Hospital, Reading, 1914-18. Her name does not appear from 1929 to 1944 and there could be any number of reasons why she chose not to register during those years. In 1944 she appears again and her address is given as Scio House, Portsmouth Road, Roehampton, London SW15. She appears in 1946 and 1947 at the same address. After 1947 only new nurses were included in the register. .

From family knowledge, we know that she nursed continuously. British Red Cross records find her nursing from March 1941 to June 1943 at Piper's Hill Auxiliary Hospital, near Leamington Spa, Warwickshire. In the Red Cross records, her home address at this time is given as her sister Violet's in Upper Gornal, near Dudley. Warwickshire County Record Office states that the Auxiliary Hospital was located at Piper's Hill Farm in the village of Bishop's Itchington.

Piper's Hill Auxiliary Hospital, Bishop's Itchington, during World War Two. Courtesy of the Hon Mrs Daphne Lakin

The Hon Mrs Daphne Lakin found this photo of Sister Emmeline Dann playing croquet with some of the patients at Piper's Hill Auxiliary Hospital. Mrs Lakin told me that her father-in-law Harry Lakin loaned the Red Cross Piper's Hill in 1940 for use as an Auxiliary Hospital. He moved out of the house and she was asked to run the hospital. At the time she was nursing at the Warneford Hospital in Leamington Spa and found the proposition "a little daunting". She was only twenty-one at the time, but: "It all happened. Our staff consisted of Matron, Sister Dann and 2 or 3 VADs. On the Administrative side, myself and Sergeant Wier. We had 32 or 36 beds. Our patients were Army or Air Force – and very occasionally Navy – convalescents and usually they were quite reluctant to be discharged!"

By the Second World War the British Red Cross and Order of St John had regrouped under the name of the Joint War Organisation and, initially, provided auxiliary homes and hospitals for officers. By 1940, the War Office approached the Joint War Organisation for assistance in providing beds for other ranks. Most of the residences for these beds were in private occupation, which created an atmosphere more conducive to recovery than that of an institution. Later, some Auxiliary Hospitals admitted civilian casualties, and some specialised (e.g. for orthopaedic cases).

Emmeline nursed and lived at Scio House, Roehampton, from 1944 until she retired. Scio House, overlooking Putney Heath, was built in 1842 and in 1925 became a Red Cross Hospital. It later became an

Emmeline in Red Cross uniform 1946

ex-servicemen's home, closing only a short while before it was purchased by property developers and demolished in 1982 despite severe local protest. The Hospital Year Book 1937 refers to Scio House as a Hospital for Officers.

During my childhood, when Emmeline came to stay, she and I would have a good time. For example, going on the Big Wheel at the annual visiting summer fair on the Den at Teignmouth. And we would eat fish and chips out of newspaper walking along the Promenade: very daring in those days!

I remember Aunt Emmeline living and nursing at Scio House. In my teens in the late 1940s, I visited her at Scio House and witnessed the warm respect in which she was held. She was nursing and caring for officers who were severely wounded in the Second World War. I would like to know more of her nursing experiences. When we are young, we do not think to ask.

I have two paintings by officers who painted them as part of their therapy and which they gave to Emmeline. One was created not long before its painter died. It is of a deep pool surrounded by dark green tall trees: it has a foreboding atmosphere.

After I left home and during the years I was raising my family, she would pop over for a couple of days when she could.

After Emmeline retired, she bought a small flat at Ardmore Lane, Buckhurst Hill, one borough away from where her sister Lily and some of her family lived at Woodford Green on the Epping Forest side of Greater London. Emmeline lived in Buckhurst Hill for the rest of her life and, as long as she was able, often visited Lily.

Emmeline on a visit to see me in Oxford 1957. She had arthritis in her knees but was determined to walk along the footpath at Port Meadow. Here she is on her way back to our small flat on Southmoor Road, resting on her stick

Emmeline furnished her flat with post-Second World War 'Utility' furniture[1], a few pieces of which I still have. It was strongly made. When I remarried in 1979, I still had Emmeline's Utility wardrobe. Occasionally, it would squeak open in the night and we would say: "Hello, Emmeline!"

Emmeline had to manage modestly in retirement. She did her best to enjoy life but missed nursing and the companionship of living-in. She was used to institutional life and found it difficult to motivate and organise her solo life. Nursing had been her passion. Dorothy helped Emmeline at the time she was establishing her own flat: a very new experience for her. She continued going to Devon for holidays with Dorothy and Gilbert for some years.

Emmeline was occasionally ill in the later years of her life, and Dorothy would sometimes go and stay with her to assist.

Emmeline died at Whipps Cross Hospital, Leytonstone, on 22nd September 1967 after a heart attack.

---

[1] Because of shortage of essential materials after the Second World War, the Government laid down standards for the manufacture of furniture, leading to limited designs and plain finishes. But the furniture was well made and lasted.

11. ARTHUR GORDON DANN

Arthur Gordon was born in 1890/91 and died at home, aged nineteen on October 28th 1910, although his family Memorial Card, reproduced below, gives the date as October 29th. He died at Norfolk Villas, St Leonard's Road, this property later being numbered as 76, St Leonard's Road. Arthur's father, Robert, was the 'informant' of the same address.

Dorothy, and her sisters, never mentioned Arthur in conversation except in general terms. For example, when they mentioned that both their brothers died young. Dorothy does not mention him in her own writing in Part 2. May, Maud and Daisy were children when their first brother died in 1894; May would have been twelve, Maud around eight and Daisy seven.

In 1910, when Arthur Gordon died, most of his sisters were still living at home. The twins, Lily and Violet were still in their mid-teens and Dorothy was ten. Emmeline and Daisy were still at home and almost certainly May was working from home. The family home must have been very crowded especially with the constraints of nursing a sick young man. The inscriptions on his Memorial Card suggest that he had endured a lot.

He died of a dropsy type illness.

Arthur's
Memorial
Card

> ### In Loving Remembrance
> OF
> ## ARTHUR GORDON DANN,
> *Who passed to the Higher Life, 29th October, 1910,*
> **AGED 19 YEARS.**
>
> " Out of great tribulation to everlasting joy."
>
> " Until the day break and the shadows flee away"—
> Farewell !

I am the youngest of all my cousins. I asked some of my older cousins if they could tell me anything about Arthur Gordon. Edna found his Memorial Card and a photo which she is sure must be him.

But nothing came to light that offered any further detail. Maybe it takes a leap in imagination to think oneself into those very different times, when premature death was still not unusual and in which an immense amount of physical and emotional work was needed to ensure that the living were cared for on a daily basis. It was simply not possible to place daily life on hold to dwell on misfortune.

In working with groups of elders on their life stories, I have sometimes heard similar surprise from participants that nothing was known about one of their parents' younger siblings who died young. Such a sibling was not discussed among family members after the funeral day.

Arthur, date unknown

12. LILY MILDRED DANN

My cousin Margaret prepared her mother Lily's family tree and it is reproduced in this chapter. It is very impressive.

Lily was a twin with Violet.

Lily took a secretarial course after leaving school. During the First World War, she was in the WAAC [Women's Auxiliary Army Corps] like her twin sister. Lily spent part of the First World War in France doing administrative work.

When Lily and Victor Palmer married, she converted to Roman Catholicism. Victor was working for Sheen and Ward, Publishers, in London. He lost a leg due to a motorcycle accident before he was married. By the time of the Second World War he was running a Timber Merchant's business and was active in the Home Guard throughout the War.

Lily and Victor with their children 1946. Left to right: Ursula, Gabrielle, Michael and Margaret

Family of Lily Mildred Dann

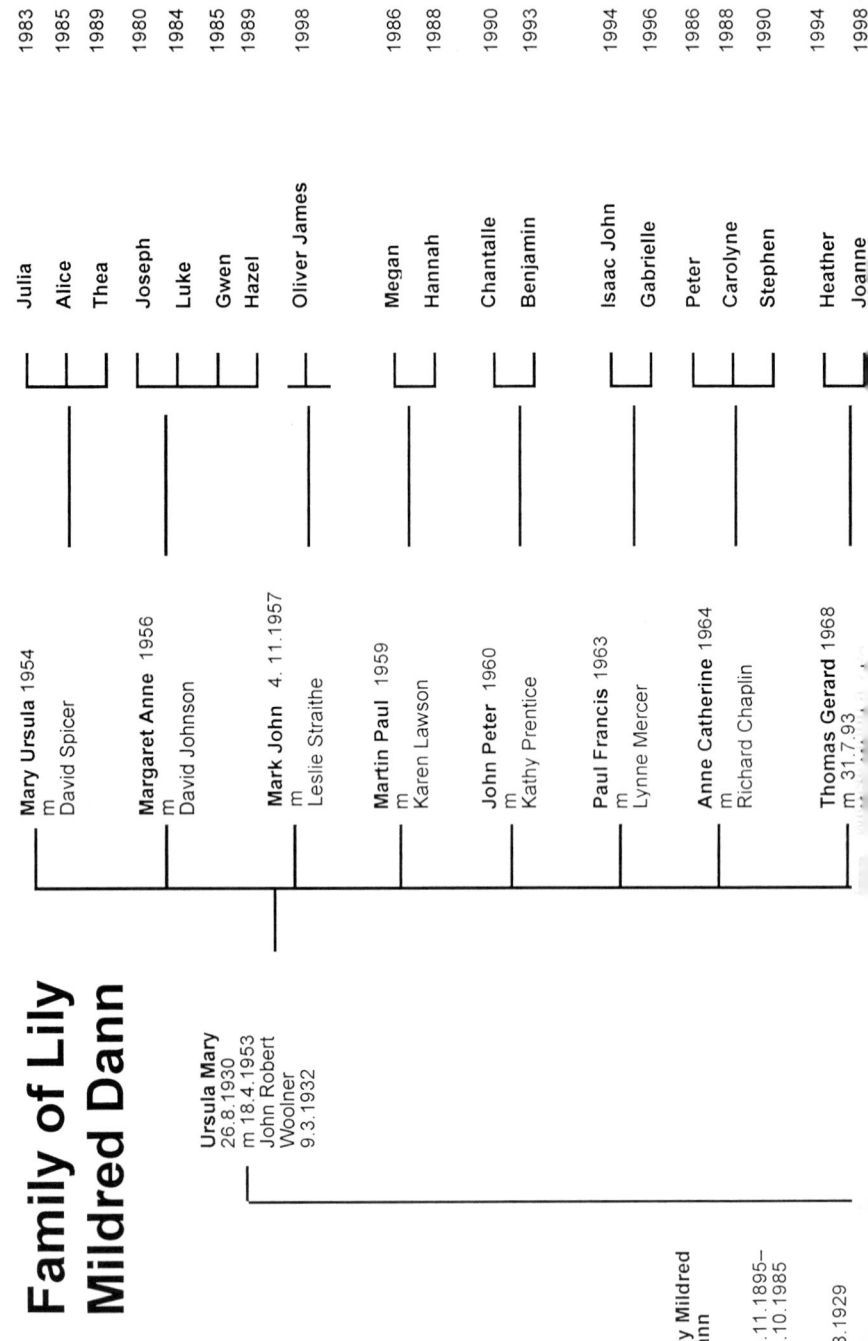

Lily Mildred Dann
30.11.1895–13.10.1985
m
3.8.1929

Ursula Mary
26.8.1930
m 18.4.1953
John Robert Woolner
9.3.1932

Mary Ursula 1954
m David Spicer
— Julia 1983
— Alice 1985
— Thea 1989

Margaret Anne 1956
m David Johnson
— Joseph 1980
— Luke 1984
— Gwen 1985
— Hazel 1989

Mark John 4. 11.1957
m Leslie Straithe
— Oliver James 1998

Martin Paul 1959
m Karen Lawson
— Megan 1986
— Hannah 1988

John Peter 1960
m Kathy Prentice
— Chantalle 1990
— Benjamin 1993

Paul Francis 1963
m Lynne Mercer
— Isaac John 1994
— Gabrielle 1996

Anne Catherine 1964
m Richard Chaplin
— Peter 1986
— Carolyne 1988
— Stephen 1990

Thomas Gerard 1968
m 31.7.93
— Heather 1994
— Joanne 1998

Victor Francis Palmer
28.6.1898 - 27.1.1976

- Michael John 9.3.69
  m 26.9.1994
  Susan Keeble
  - Emma Jane 21.4.1997
  - Hannah 23.3.1994
- **Margaret Monica**
  7.11.32
  m 21.5.1966
  Kevin John Healey
  7.1.32
  - **Peter Mark** 22.8.1971
    p. Julie Hall
    - Lauren 13.1.2003
    - William 4.6.1992
  - **Helen Marcella** 18.7.1973
    m 3.12.1994
    Paul Gray
    - Rosanna 20.4.1995
    - George 16.7.1999
    - Jonathan 3.3.1995
  - **Frances Caroline** 19.4.1976
    m
    Robert Swales
    - Benjamin 8.1.1999
    - Lily 23.1.2001
- **Michael Victor**
  25.6.1935
  m 14.9.1977
  Jerri Cronkhite
  div.1990
  — No issue
  - **Joseph Victor** 6.4.1961
  - **Stephen Francis** 5.3.1962
    m 16.9.1989
    Elizabeth Welham
    - Luke Martin 4.1.1992
    - Connor Michael 9.2.1994
  - **David John** 6.4.1963
    m 20.2.88
    Susan Whelan
    - James Michael 3.10.1990
    - William Thomas 20.5.1992
    - Michael David 23.12.1993
    - Harry 28.10.2001
- **Gabrielle Anne**
  25.6.1935
  m 12.5.1960
  Deric Clifford Evans
  21.8.1925
  - **Catherine Anne** 30.7.1964
    m 30.5.92
    Simon Batten
    - Bryn 22.5.2001
    - Elenydd 6.11.2002
    - Daniel Thomas 4.6.1993
  - **Agnes Mary** 27.10.1966
    m 11.5.1991
    Philip William Sutton
    - Peter Nicholas 23.12.1994
    - Benedict Michael 22.8.1997
    - Anna 12.11.2002
  - **John Thomas** 25.6.1970
    m 1.8.1998
    Rachel Ottevanger
    - Isaac Francis 4.6.1999
    - Thomas 13.4.2001
    - Reuben 7.11.2003
  - **Margaret Myfanwy** 27.7.1972
    m
    Michael O'Reilly
    - Huw 29.7.2003

41

For some years, Margaret spent at least a week each summer with our family in Teignmouth and we, being teenagers under two years apart in age, enjoyed time together.

Lily and my mother kept in touch regularly and met as opportunity afforded. In 1980, Dorothy lived with me and my children in Teddington for some months before we moved to Warwick. During these months, cousin Edna from nearby Walton-on-Thames occasionally took Dorothy to see Lily at Woodford Green. She had lived there for many years.

Lily and Dorothy were both skilled and fast knitters and my mind boggles to think how many garments, shawls, bedspreads and other things they knitted in their lifetimes, and how many rugs they made: these activities being conducted whilst usually doing something else.

Coincidences so often happen in life. When I lived in Nottingham 1965 - 76, one of my friends, Kathy Austen, was a near neighbour. In the course of conversation, we discovered that her husband, Joe, was son of a sister of Victor Palmer's. Dorothy remembered bouncing Joe on her knee when he was a baby!

Lily was one of those family members whom I felt I knew really well, yet we never had opportunity to spend much time together. Shortly before she died, with obvious difficulty she wrote to me saying how glad she was that I was at last making progress (I had been paralysed through a medical injury some eighteen months earlier in 1984). She said: "I pray for you every night and I expect others do as well. You certainly have been suffering but everything comes to an end."

Then with the good humour that was her hallmark, she commented that – because of arthritis and her head being bowed – she couldn't see if she looked beautiful! And: "Gabrielle and Derek paid me a surprise visit yesterday and brought me two little miniature pink roses in a pot, some chocolate and a flask of coffee. It was such a pleasant surprise when they walked in. It took them one-and-a-half hours from Woodford. It was a lovely day."

Because of frailty, Lily was then living with her daughter Margaret in Newmarket in Suffolk, having left her home of many years at 74, Broadmead Road, Woodford Green. She was happy with Margaret and Kevin. Although she had a large direct family to think about, Lily's interest and concern extended to include others. For example, leading up to the first anniversary of my mother Dorothy's death, she wrote the following note:

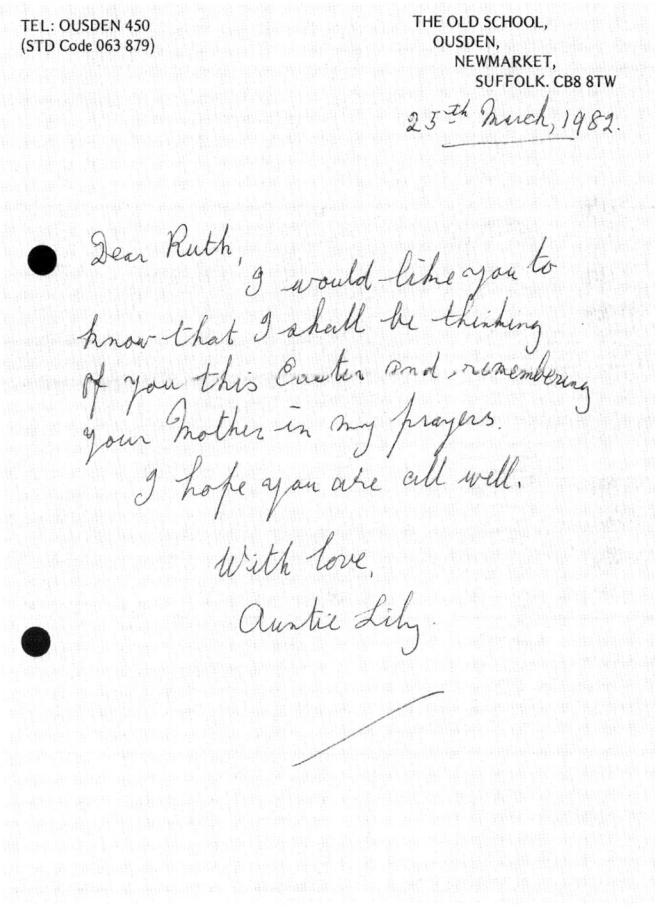

TEL: OUSDEN 450
(STD Code 063 879)

THE OLD SCHOOL,
OUSDEN,
NEWMARKET,
SUFFOLK. CB8 8TW

25th March, 1982.

Dear Ruth,
I would like you to know that I shall be thinking of you this Easter and remembering your mother in my prayers.
I hope you are all well.

With love,
Auntie Lily.

Lily outlived Dorothy by four-and-a-half years and was the last of her siblings to die.

13. VIOLET MABEL DANN

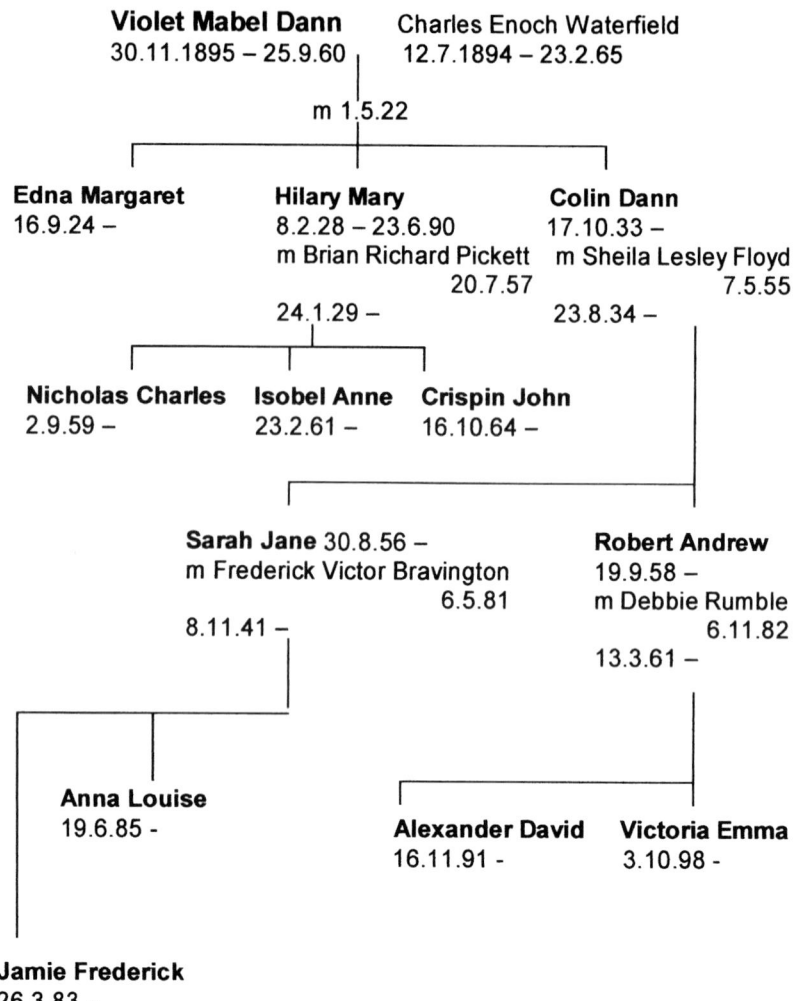

Violet Mabel Dann
30.11.1895 – 25.9.60

Charles Enoch Waterfield
12.7.1894 – 23.2.65

m 1.5.22

Edna Margaret
16.9.24 –

Hilary Mary
8.2.28 – 23.6.90
m Brian Richard Pickett
20.7.57
24.1.29 –

Colin Dann
17.10.33 –
m Sheila Lesley Floyd
7.5.55
23.8.34 –

Nicholas Charles
2.9.59 –

Isobel Anne
23.2.61 –

Crispin John
16.10.64 –

Sarah Jane 30.8.56 –
m Frederick Victor Bravington
6.5.81
8.11.41 –

Robert Andrew
19.9.58 –
m Debbie Rumble
6.11.82
13.3.61 –

Anna Louise
19.6.85 -

Alexander David
16.11.91 -

Victoria Emma
3.10.98 -

Jamie Frederick
26.3.83 –

Cousin Edna thinks the name Waterfield derived from French stock and probably the town of Vatierville. Her mother Violet (twin of Lily) was, says Edna, the 'naughty' twin.

Violet told Edna that, when the Dann home at 76, St Leonard's Road, Hythe, was requisitioned by the Army in the First World War, the family moved to Stade Street. The house was on the corner of an unmade tree-lined road and it was bigger than their own home. So Martha Dann sent Robert out to buy some second-hand chairs. Instead, he came back with a terrestrial globe!

Violet went for nurses' training to a hospital in Gillingham, North Kent, but was sent home because she was anaemic. For a while she worked in a Haberdasher's shop in Hythe High Street. During the First World War, she joined the WAAC [Women's Auxiliary Army Corps] and, it was during this time, she met Charles Enoch Waterfield who was posted to Hythe in the Royal Flying Corps on 1.4.1916.

His family came from Upper Gornal in the Black Country. He was one of eleven children and both his parents died within months of each other when he was ten-years-old. His parents had run a Fire Brick Works. After their death, the older siblings sold it without much benefit to the family. But his mother had left each child £1,000 (a considerable sum then) and Charles used some of his inheritance to gain an education at Dudley Grammar School.

Between school and being Called Up, he worked for the up-and-coming firm Lucas and Sons in Birmingham [now TRW Aeronautical Systems, Lucas Aerospace]. The company was a leading one in the manufacture of motor car parts and, when Charles was employed there, it was about to enter the aerospace market with a prototype for the first engine starter.

Violet and Charles made their home in Upper Gornal and, after the First World War, he set up a motor haulage firm with a fleet of lorries. Violet died of cancer, as did her younger daughter, Hilary, who was a trained Primary School teacher. She left the Midlands to

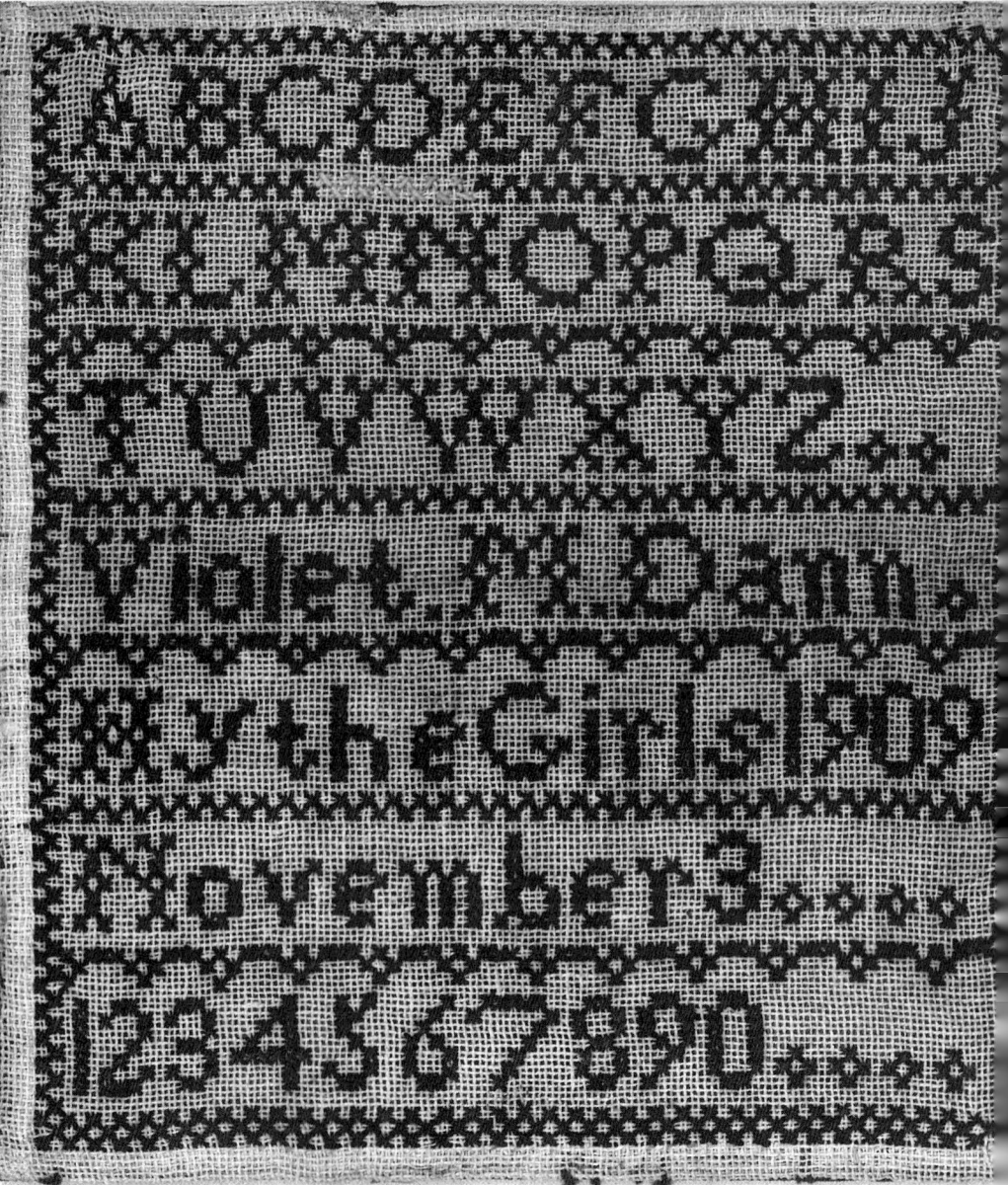

Sampler worked by Violet at Hythe Girls' School in November 1909. The stitching is in red. Although samplers have become rather taken for granted as set pieces girls once made, they involved not only considerable manual dexterity and neatness, but also a mathematical and design skill in planning stitches to fit a given space

teach in Folkestone where she met her husband, Brian. He worked in banking.

Edna remembers her mother, Violet, taking her to an Aunt Honor ('or was it Mercy') who ran a cake shop in Victoria Street, London, before World War Two. These are names also mentioned by my cousin Barbara, but I do not know exactly where they fitted in the extended family.

Edna recalls that her parents and siblings went regularly to Hythe before the Second World War. They slept in the attic at their grandparents' home at 76, St Leonard's Road, until they were elderly. Then the visiting family stayed in a house further down St Leonard's Road, run by a Miss Holland. "I look back on those times with happiness," says Edna.

Edna says Grandad Dann sat in a large wooden chair playing the banjo, playing songs like: 'One man went to mow, went to mow a meadow . . .'

Whilst her family were on holiday in Hythe, Edna recalls: "We used to picnic by the Military Canal and, one summer, Phillip [Maud's younger son], wearing immaculate white shorts, ruined them sliding down a grassy bank – he was in trouble! But we used to dress up in those days, and I have a snap of my brother Colin aged three or four sitting quite elegantly in short trousers and a frilly looking shirt. We all 'dress down' these days."

Edna spent a couple of days in Hythe with her sister Hilary before she died and they were horrified to see what had been done to the family home by way of gentrification.

Edna started working for Barclays Bank in Birmingham in 1941, later being transferred to London in the Bank's Property Division. She became PA to the Chief Architect and retired in 1980. She moved to East Grinstead and plays an active role in her extended family, especially since the death of her sister.

This was Colin's suit of the 'ghastly blue colour'. He is sitting on the gate at Leigh Bank, Teignmouth

Edna and Colin were cousins who visited our home in Teignmouth for holidays when I was growing up. It is strange what things we remember from our youth! Colin recalls my mother, Dorothy, asking if a suit he was wearing 'which on reflection was rather a ghastly blue colour' was issued by the RAF! He was staying at Teignmouth for a break while he was training in the RAF in Cornwall. He met his future wife, Lesley, in Penzance.

On one of his visits, he had a new camera and insisted on taking photos of me on The Ness promontory at Shaldon, opposite Teignmouth, at the mouth of the river Teign. I was wearing a winter coat that I had made myself. Dorothy was very clever at sewing and I grew up 'knowing' how to sew because she did.

Colin left the RAF in 1985 after some thirty-four years of service, with a variety of postings, both home and overseas. "As one gets older the opportunities for flying reduce and you become more desk bound," says Colin: "and, as is almost inevitable, a stint in the Ministry of Defence in London." Then, for eight years, he joined a firm that dealt in defence matters, retiring in 1993. Like most 'retired' people these days, he and Lesley are very busy. They live in a Wiltshire village of some 450 people.

A Waterfield wedding. Violet and Charles Waterfield's son, Flying Officer Colin Dann Waterfield marries Sheila Lesley Floyd at St John's Church, Penzance, on May 7th 1955. Left to right: Flying Officer Hall. Hilary (Colin's sister), Edna (Colin's sister), Rachel Brookes (Charles Waterfield's sister), Charles, Violet, Flying Officer Keith Shearer (best man), Colin, Lesley, Jack Daniel (Lesley's uncle), Elizabeth (Lesley's sister), Margery Floyd (Lesley's mother), Jill Allen (Lesley's sister) and Michael Daniel (Jack Daniel's son).

Violet and Charles with their daughters, Edna and Hilary (at the back)

Whilst on holiday in Teignmouth c1949. Violet's elder daughter, Edna, walking along the seafront at Torquay with Dorothy. At seaside towns after the War, roving photographers started to make a living from photographing the increasing number of summer holidaymakers. As 'locals' we were always being asked if we wanted our photo taken and, for some years, our family album contains evidence that occasionally we said: "Yes"! Not many people had their own cameras then. Or, if they did, it would usually be a Brownie Box camera, and not carried about a great deal. Our family had a Brownie Box camera that took some of the informal photos in this book in the later 1940s – early 1960s

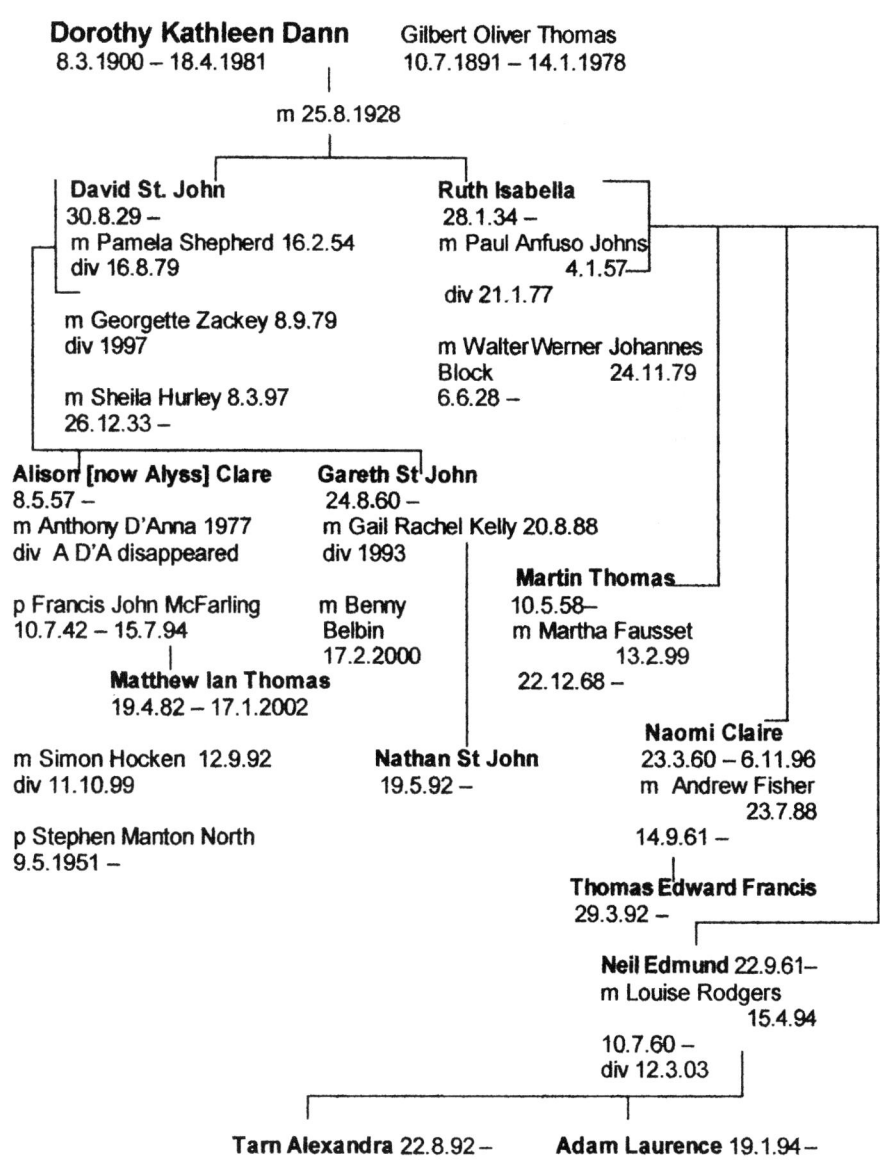

Dorothy Kathleen Dann
8.3.1900 – 18.4.1981

Gilbert Oliver Thomas
10.7.1891 – 14.1.1978

m 25.8.1928

David St. John
30.8.29 –
m Pamela Shepherd 16.2.54
div 16.8.79

m Georgette Zackey 8.9.79
div 1997

m Sheila Hurley 8.3.97
26.12.33 –

Ruth Isabella
28.1.34 –
m Paul Anfuso Johns
4.1.57
div 21.1.77

m Walter Werner Johannes
Block   24.11.79
6.6.28 –

Alison [now Alyss] Clare
8.5.57 –
m Anthony D'Anna 1977
div A D'A disappeared

p Francis John McFarling
10.7.42 – 15.7.94

Gareth St John
24.8.60 –
m Gail Rachel Kelly 20.8.88
div 1993

m Benny
Belbin
17.2.2000

Martin Thomas
10.5.58–
m Martha Fausset
13.2.99
22.12.68 –

Matthew Ian Thomas
19.4.82 – 17.1.2002

m Simon Hocken 12.9.92
div 11.10.99

p Stephen Manton North
9.5.1951 –

Nathan St John
19.5.92 –

Naomi Claire
23.3.60 – 6.11.96
m Andrew Fisher
23.7.88
14.9.61 –

Thomas Edward Francis
29.3.92 –

Neil Edmund 22.9.61–
m Louise Rodgers
15.4.94
10.7.60 –
div 12.3.03

Tarn Alexandra 22.8.92 –

Adam Laurence 19.1.94 –

Dorothy Kathleen was born at the turn of the 20th Century and was the youngest of Robert and Martha's nine children. Seven were girls and survived into adult life. The two boys died young, one aged ten and the other aged nineteen. In Part 2, Dorothy tells her own story of childhood and young adult life.

Dorothy ended her autobiography at the time she married in 1928, which itself is an interesting statement. This warm woman tells her story clearly but within a style of constraint she learned to exercise in her life after marriage. She does not mention many names. But, importantly, she needed to place that period of her independent life on the record. Maybe she realised that her life illustrated one important strand of social history.

Dorothy's young life was discussed occasionally in my growing-up years but only in the most general terms: for example, as being 'very happy'. She discussed it more as she grew older. She kept contact with her Hythe roots all her life, although the last members of her family to leave did so in the Second World War. Our family took one post-War holiday in Hythe, together with Dorothy's sister Emmeline. I visited Hythe for the next time in 1995.

Upon marriage, the Marriage Bar denied her the job she loved. It was one in which she excelled. The prospect of a Headship was open to her at the time of marriage, had that been her choice instead of marriage.

As we will see in Part 3, after marriage Dorothy shouldered the overriding responsibility to create a harmonious and interesting home life, often in difficult circumstances (as in the early years of World War Two). Her innately generous personality, and the gift from her birth family of tolerance and knowledge that achievement was possible, led her – at that time in history – to accept the role of Gilbert's wife on his terms. This meant being someone who should master all domestic practicalities, skills and circumstances with little thought for her own emotional comfort.

Although Gilbert could appreciate a teacher's skill (as shown in his poem *Infant Teacher*[1]), he did not recognize how profoundly Dorothy's life changed upon marriage. When I was adult and a mother myself, she would occasionally mention how lonely she was in the early years after giving up teaching. She never blamed Gilbert.

As a young woman in my early twenties, I sometimes challenged Gilbert's ideas as they affected Dorothy. I longed to see him offer her some visible appreciation. He would tell me that it was the highest role in life for a woman to run a home and family. End of matter! He *did* value Dorothy's skills but he seldom offered any affirmation of them, and he had no idea of the constraints he placed on her. She offered him huge encouragement and appreciation, both privately and publicly.

Research for this book has caused me to wonder why Dorothy and Gilbert's direct family experienced more divorces than other branches of the family (although there are a few broken relationships which do not show up on the extended family trees seen earlier).

This is not the place to discuss this question in any length because this is Dorothy's story and not that of her descendants. If she had any part in shaping how following generations made decisions, it was her unerring acceptance that Gilbert's needs, preferences, choices and decisions were paramount. This has probably reverberated down two generations, not always along gender lines.

As I have grown older and experienced the various stages of life, I can see more clearly not only what Dorothy achieved but also what she lost. That loss – its reasons and her response – became part of my brother's and my inheritance: what we have each done with it has differed. Our responses reflect what parental values we each

---

[1] *Collected Poems* by Gilbert Thomas [David & Charles/Allen & Unwin. 1969].

internalised, our response to the culture of our own time and our own personalities. For example, in early adult life I – like Dorothy – slipped into the role of believing it was my responsibility to make everyday things 'all right' and worried inordinately when that was not possible. Eventually, I accepted that I was not the only party to have responsibilities!

But this is not to cast any 'blame' on Dorothy. If our parents do the best they can within the constraints of their lives and times, we have much for which to be grateful. Not all parents do their best. And, if either of my parents was the more responsible for any 'reverberations down the generations', then it was Gilbert. He never questioned his attitudes. They were right! He chose not to be involved in day-to-day decision-making. So any dissatisfaction over the outcome of the decisions made landed unfairly on Dorothy!

And, of course, each generation introduces different, complementary or sometimes reinforcing reverberations from new members joining the family.

In my view, Gilbert and Dorothy's marriage, whilst enduring with considerable strengths, was not quite as trouble-free as Gilbert chose to believe or as Dorothy tried tirelessly to make it. Their life together and our family life had much to commend it. But unspoken tensions are powerful.

Gilbert, in different times, would undoubtedly have had a different view of marriage. He genuinely believed he was acting in Dorothy's best interests and that he understood what those were. He left an interesting interpretation of his ideas about parenthood, and those he thought to be Dorothy's, in his book *Master-Light: Letters to David* [George Allen & Unwin. 1932].

On my seventeenth birthday, he slipped a poem under my bedroom door in the early morning. It was later published as *For Ruth Isabella*. The second verse read:

Seventeen? Yet also seven, my dear,
  And even seventy you are.
Child, girl, wife, mother all seem here:
  Hints of the granny too.

That did not portray my total destiny!

Although our family has been challenged with some difficult and sad events, not least the untimely deaths of my beloved daughter Naomi from cancer and great-nephew Matthew from an involuntary heroin overdose, it has survived. And the 'step' members are a very important and positive part of it.

Not shown on the above family tree are the following step-relations. Walter Block, my husband, has a son, Martin John (2.3.61 –) and a daughter Ruth [Ru-tee] Anna (20.6.66 –) from his first marriage. The first year Walter and I were together, we asked our children if they wanted to go on holiday with us. All five said 'yes,' which was great. The only snag was that Walter's son and my elder son are both called Martin! For people we met, that was a trifle baffling! And my step-daughter, like me, was Ruth. Some years later, she adopted the African form of the name, Ru-tee. Dorothy grew very fond of Walter and this affection was reciprocated: they had a lot of fun together.

My widowed son-in-law, Andrew Fisher, has a partner, Jane Oldfield. Jane has four children, Keeley (8.4.82 –), Lee (5.4.85 –), Louennie (26.1.89 –) and Bethany (18.2.94 –).

On June 27th 1987, Martin John Block married Karen Wallace (5.4.62 –) and they have three daughters, Francesca Rhianon (30.3.89 –), Stephanie Roseanne (3.4.91 –) and Gabriella Megan (2.8.93 –).

Ru-tee Block has a partner, Marc Faupel (21.3. 69 –).

Benny Thomas (nee Belbin) has a son, Richard (22.3.91 –), from her first marriage.

Dorothy's parents when Dorothy was teaching in Hythe in the early 1920s. Robert Dann, pipe in mouth, at work potting plants in the doorway of the greenhouse at 76, St Leonard's Road, and Martha Dann taking a well-earned rest with a book in the garden

PART 2

BROKEN EGGS CAN'T SING*

DOROTHY'S OWN ACCOUNT OF HER LIFE 1900-28

by Dorothy Thomas (nee Dann)

* This was the title Dorothy gave her manuscript

Studio photo of Dorothy around one-year old

15. EARLIEST MEMORIES: HYTHE LIFEBOAT

A gale howled across Romney Marsh. The rain pounded on the window. Above the noise of the storm, the lifeboat maroon summoned its crew. Soon the men would be running past the house, battling against wind and rain to reach the Lifeboat House not many yards away.

I knew, if I kept awake, I should hear the crew return if all had gone well. But I fell asleep – until roused by a commotion about the house. Going into another room, I saw two small tousled heads above the blankets and four scared dark eyes. My mother came into the room, carrying a tray with hot drinks, and soon the mother of the children followed. The crew were taking the rescued father and other men to their own homes. They had left the mother and her young children at the first house where they knew they would be cared for. This was one of my earliest memories.

Photo of the Hythe Lifeboat and its crew when Dorothy was a child.
Courtesy of the Image Resource Unit, Royal National Lifeboat Institution

Our home in Hythe was not a big one, but the open spaces all round gave it an added dimension. I always felt free. For me the Lifeboat House was a magnet. Its big doors were often left wide open. One or two fishermen would be working nearby, mending their nets or making new ones. These, when finished, were thrown into a large copper to be tanned. As the steam arose, an acrid smell blew across the beach. A black hut stood near where the herrings hung in rows, being cured into bloaters.

With sisters and friends, I often went into the lifeboat house. There were no restrictions, so long as we respected the gear and everything else that was left in perfect order, ready for the sudden call that might at any time come from a vessel in distress. If one of the crew was working in the lifeboat and invited us to come up the steps to join him, I felt I was about to enter holy ground. The crew's yellow oilskins and sou'westers hung in a row on the wall. Near the door, on a large blackboard, was a list of the wrecks that had called for help and the numbers of the rescued. The dates were given. I knew the list by heart, but never passed the board without reading it again.

The Hythe Lifeboat Station Dorothy knew (and as shown on the map on pages 64/65), but this photo is of a slightly later date, 1929. Courtesy of the Image Resource Unit, Royal National Lifeboat Institution

Benvenue was among the ships named. I felt nostalgic when, not long ago, I heard the wreck of the *Benvenue*[1] spoken of on the radio. I seemed to grow up with the story of this disaster near our beach. So vivid was the picture of it all that even now I can't quite believe I wasn't there to enter into the excitement. The locals picked up nuts in great quantities. One aged fisherman told me that his family harvested several pillowcases full. These they kept under the bed.

Now, we are all accustomed to the diesel engine. What grand seamanship and courage did those old-time fishermen who manned the lifeboat display! With what almost superhuman effort they wielded their oars when sails could not be used! How I loved to watch them set out! As the crew held up their oars at forty-five degrees, the boat ran down over the greased runners, then – with a great splash – into the sea.

To witness the determination of the men in a South West gale filled my young heart with pride. Fear mingled with pride on the evening when one member of the crew was absent. The cox called for a volunteer, and my father climbed into the boat.

The new Lifeboat was resplendent upon the beach[2], waiting to be christened. When the bottle was broken over the bow, I took it for granted that the liquid was water. When told it was champagne – and what a price! – I thought the grown-ups were crazy.

One day every summer, the lifeboat was drawn on its carriage from the landward-looking door of its house. Four horses were then harnessed to it: or were there six? All the sailors' and fishermen's

---

1 The *Benvenue* crew were rescued by the Hythe Lifeboat at its second attempt in November 1891. The full report that appeared in the *Hythe Reporter* about this event can be read on www.hythelive.com/history/benvenue, together with a reminder that the Hythe Lifeboat was only 37 x 8 feet and had merely a sail and twelve oars. There were, of course, no telephones or radios.
2 It was launched in 1910.

children were taken for a ride through the town and along the coast road. If there were any vacant seats, those of us whose fathers were not sailors or fishermen went aboard. There was always room, but oh! The suspense as I stood below waiting to hear one of the crew call: 'Come up.'

So we 'sailed' along the road. The crew in their navy jerseys and long red woolly hats walked beside the boat, shaking collecting boxes. These were miniature lifeboats. Three miles there and three miles back: did ever journey seem more pleasantly long? Memory does not register any wet days.

When we returned, the lifeboat was launched for a quick practice. We waited for it to come back: then all hands on the capstan. Round and round we went until the loved boat was in her house again, the crew's yellow oilskins and sou'westers once more hanging on the wall, and everything in 'apple-pie' order for the next call.

To me the lifeboat was invincible. Many years later, looking at a newspaper picture of the Rye lifeboat, washed up on the shore, turned upside down, her men all drowned, I felt the impossible had happened.

16. FISHERMEN AND COASTGUARDS

Whenever I passed the fishermen on the rough shingly road between our house and the beach, and saw them carrying loaves and other provisions to their smacks, ready for the night's fishing, one thing perplexed me. If I were a heathen looking for something to worship, I should without doubt choose air, moving air. My environment in early years may account for this. I could not understand how men who lived so much in the open air could be happy in what seemed to me an oppressively stuffy little cabin.

I had the same feeling when with a friend I visited the home of our Sunday School Teacher. Her father was the gardener at Saltwood Castle: their cottage stood nearby. To the eye, everything about that cottage attracted me, not least the proximity of the Castle itself. Never, I think, have I needed to use more self-control than when sitting at tea in that delightful cottage. I was ten. Large flowering geraniums completely covered the window, leaving us in semi-darkness and keeping out any fresh air. The door was shut and, there, outside were the great walls of the Castle. I still marvel how people who work in the open air can be happy to live, at home, under such – to me – stifling conditions.

The coastguards, no less than the fishermen, were our friends. With never failing regularity they began their work early in the morning. The first sound I heard when I awoke was the raking of the paths that led to the two long rows of their houses and of the smaller ones that divided their perfectly tended vegetable gardens. With the rake on Monday mornings came out the pails of whitewash with the big brushes standing in them. A four-foot wall enclosed the Chief Officer's house, which was just opposite our home, and the sailors' quarters and their gardens, making a little world apart. Both sides of this wall were whitewashed every week and the large stones that edged the paths were given their white covering also, every one of them.

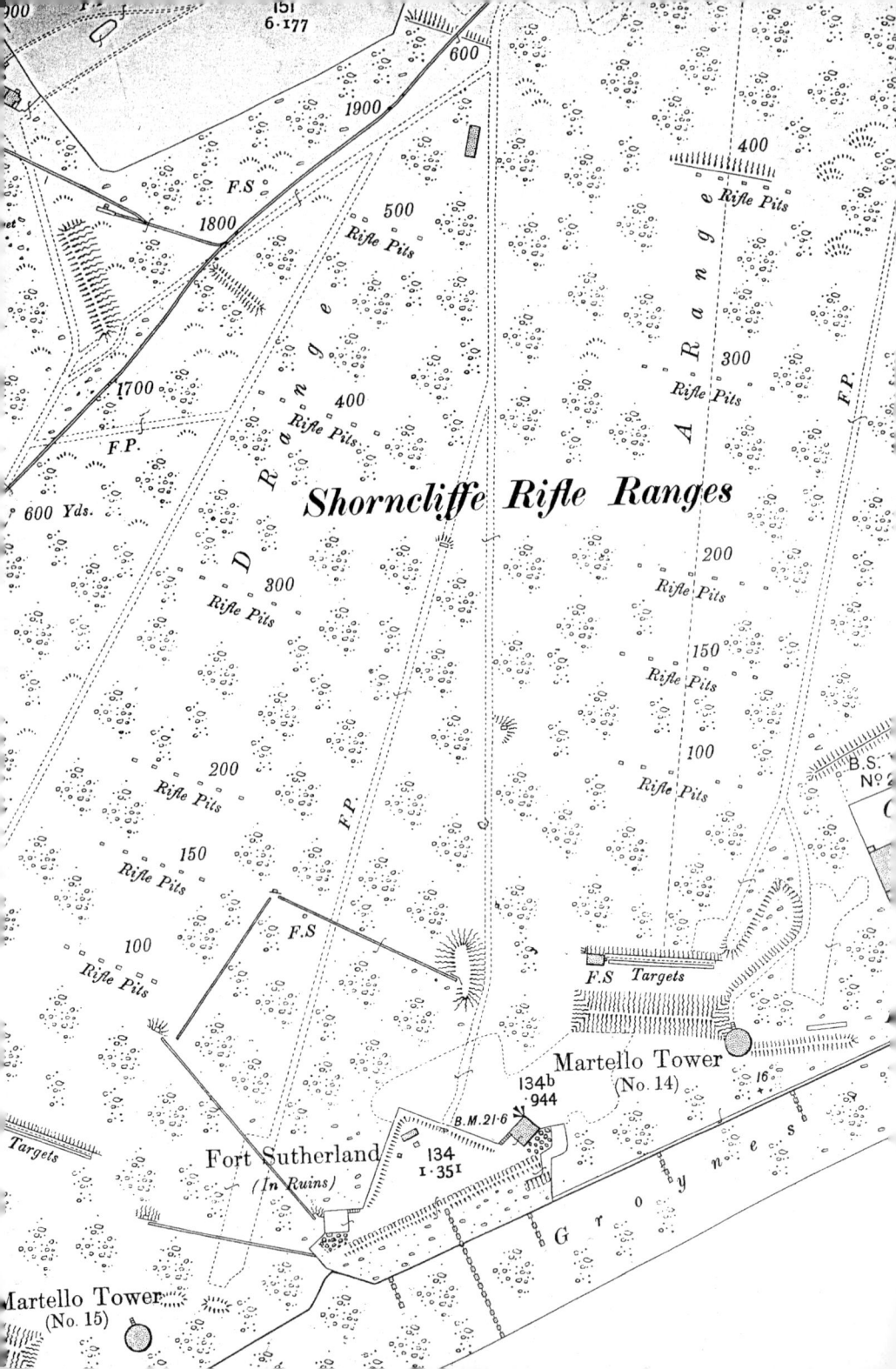

151
6·177

600

1900

F.S
1800

500

Rifle Pits

400

Rifle Pits

400

Rifle Pits

Rifle Pits

300

Rifle Pits

200

Rifle Pits

150

Rifle Pits

100

Rifle Pits

1700

F.P.

600 Yds.

300

Rifle Pits

200

Rifle Pits

150

Rifle Pits

100

Rifle Pits

Shorncliffe Rifle Ranges

D   R a n g e

A   R a n g e

F.P.

F.P.

F.S

F.S Targets

B.S.
Nᵒ

Martello Tower
(No. 14)

134b
·944

B.M. 21·6

134
1·35¹

16

Fort Sutherland
(*In Ruins*)

Targets

G r o y n e s

Targets

Martello Tower
(No. 15)

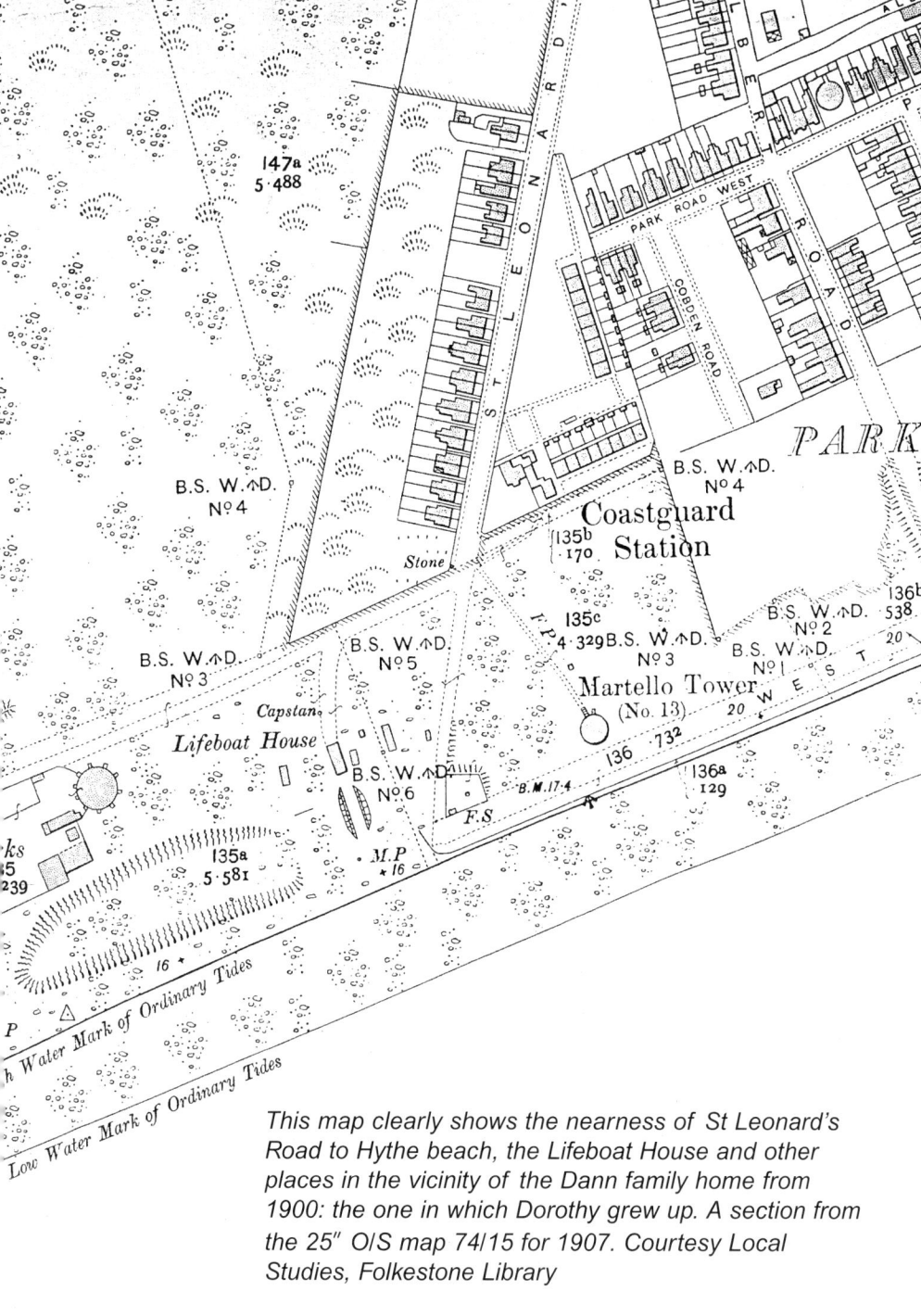

This map clearly shows the nearness of St Leonard's Road to Hythe beach, the Lifeboat House and other places in the vicinity of the Dann family home from 1900: the one in which Dorothy grew up. A section from the 25″ O/S map 74/15 for 1907. Courtesy Local Studies, Folkestone Library

With long big swabs the yards in front of the men's homes received their twice-weekly cleaning. With bare feet, their wide sailors' trousers rolled up, the men with practised rhythm dipped the swab into the bucket and, with a twist of the arm, would turn the swab from side to side, slowly moving backwards, taking the bucket with them until all the area had been washed over.

Their lookout hut stood at the end of the Parade. Made of wood it braved the high seas that sent the waves right over it. Regularly the men walked up and down the road to take over their hours of duty. The hut was never left unattended.

What a kindly group of men these sailors were, always busy, never in a hurry, friends indeed to the children who were fortunate enough to live near them.

The little lookout hut held a store of knowledge. The walls were covered with maritime charts, and there were pictures of many ships sailing the seven seas. The big coloured chart of all the nations' flags had its place just to the right of the little circle through which the coastguard put his spyglass to see what was passing up and down the channel.

During World War One, drawings of different sea-mines and other necessary information were posted up. The small white flags used for Morse signalling were on the shelf. One of the men's duties was to walk along the shore: that shore with Romney Marsh behind it, which had been the scene of so much smuggling in former years. Pattens[1] stood in a corner of the hut, to be used for walking over the stony beach.

It was the coast guards who jumped down the wall and came to our assistance when a too-hastily put-up tent blew over. They generally walked off with the first prize at the annual Venetian Fete on the

---

[1] A clog or overshoe mounted on an iron ring etc for keeping the shoes out of the mud or wet. *Cassell's New English Dictionary.* 1949.

Royal Military Canal. When not on duty, their deft fingers were making rugs or doing some other handwork. On Guy Fawkes Night, the sailors built an enormous bonfire. After it had died down, they dug potatoes from their gardens and, after washing them under the pump, would then roast them for us in the hot ashes.

One day the man on duty called us from our tent to come up on the Parade. 'Hurry, hurry!' he shouted. When we reached him, he stooped to our level and, guiding our eyes with his outstretched arm, showed us a small object moving toward our coast. It was Bleriot's plane making its historic crossing from France[2].

"Now," he said: "you can always say you saw the first aeroplane cross the English Channel." I was much disappointed. I had thought an aeroplane would look like a huge cloud moving in the sky. This might have been a seagull.

Every morning the flag was hoisted, and I was often allowed to lower it at sunset. Special flags were flown for great occasions. Many flags flew in the wind on Trafalgar Day, repeating Nelson's message to his men.

One of the coastguards and his family were moving to a new station. A large vessel was anchored some distance out at sea. Making several journeys, a boat took all the family's belongings to the waiting ship. Finally, with all the farewells over, the sailor, his wife and children stepped into the boat and were rowed out. I stood by the edge of the sea, watching the boat grow smaller and smaller. I felt miserable. The name of the new station didn't help: Land's End.

The station at Hythe, like many another, is now closed. No friendly sailor stands on guard by the hut. The once gleaming walls are dingy. No longer can a child see on May Day the sailors put the white tops on their caps and know that summer, with all its fun, is very near.

---

2   On July 25th 1909, Louis Bleriot, French aviator and inventor, was the first person to fly the English Channel.

One of the great pleasures of summer was the annual visit of a circus – not for the show put on in the afternoons, but for the procession of animals that passed our house on the way to the sea. It came by at six o'clock in the morning, headed by many horses, including some lovely piebald and the smallest of Shetland ponies, two camels (or were they dromedaries?), two elephants, performing dogs on a lead, two llamas walking side by side lifting their feet daintily as they passed by: and the rest.

When the procession ended, we ran up to the Parade to watch them in the sea. All went into the water, if only to walk at the edge. Little of an elephant, ridden by its trainer and its trunk thrown back, showed when it was swimming. One thing spoiled the arrival of the circus. We were not allowed in the sea until two tides had washed the beach. The time came when, for reasons of hygiene – when there were more holidaymakers – the authorities stopped this annual trek to the beach.

17. CHILDHOOD FREEDOM

I don't think I ever planted a seed, except mustard and cress on flannel, or pulled up a single weed in our small home garden. Yet, after over half-a-century, I could draw a plan showing the exact position of every tree and shrub. I loved them all except the privet hedge. Our bathing dresses were dried on this and, in the morning before going to the beach, we shook and shook them as earwigs fell to the ground.

There was one pear tree that never set fruit, though it did have its hour. After many years, to the excitement of the family it produced a single pear. My sisters and I were told not to pick it. We watched it grow and grow into a real beauty. Then, obeying the letter rather than the spirit of our instructions, we bit into it, ate all the fruit and left the core hanging on the bough!

I had only to open a door at the end of the garden and step out on to the fringe of Romney Marsh. On the garden side of the door all was order and tidiness. On the other side the land stretched wide and open. The door faced due west. The blue clumps of viper's bugloss glistened against the sunset sky. I loved the blue-green leaves of the horned poppy with its yellow flowers. Did ever a flower, when picked, so quickly shed its petals? To sit by the gorse bushes, with the breeze carrying the sweet pineapple scent of the yellow blossom, and to hear the quiet pop, pop, pop of the buds bursting in the hot sunshine, was for me the quintessence of summer.

What a ceremony we made if we found a dead bird! I fear our feelings were not mainly for the small-feathered body. It gave us the opportunity to gather mallow, trefoil, yarrow, bladder campion, thistles, thrift, and all the other flowers growing in fields and near the shore to make a grand floral pattern for its grave. A long time would be spent searching to find a flower of exactly the right size and colour to match one in the design. Sometimes the whole pattern was given a frame of an inch or so of red ripened dock seeds. Once on my way home from the beach, I gathered a bucket full of these seeds. Taking them in through the garden door, I left them on the grass. Very soon I was asked to return them outside. Dock seeds, especially in big numbers, are not the most-welcome guests in any garden.

Back inside, I stood by two pale pink hydrangeas. A passion plant climbed high near them. The contrast between the hydrangeas and the passion flowers worried me. The hydrangeas, with their huge blousy blooms, looked the same day after day, week after week. They never changed. Death seemed to pass them by. This struck my childish mind as unfair, for the beautiful greenish-white passion flower, with its blue fringe, lived but a day. Many an early morning I stood looking at a newly opened bloom, telling myself that this one would live longer, even while I knew I should see its petals closed by late afternoon.

I found this photo in Dorothy's album. It is dated 1909. The two tall girls at the back are her twin sisters Lily and Violet. Dorothy is the girl holding the dog. The other children are friends. We get a glimpse of the freedom children had and also, as cousin Edna said, of how parents worked so hard to dress children well even when they were playing. My aunts used to refer to being dressed 'sprucely' in their young days. Children's clothes were handed down and neatly mended but always well washed and ironed

With sisters and friends, I never lacked companionship. The open space around, the Parade and the beach gave us a free world. As a child, I found it hard to understand that people could live at the seaside yet from one year's end to another never go for a walk on the Parade or spend an hour or two on the shore. The sea didn't seem to exist for them. It was a big part of my life. In winter, I found comfort in the beam from Cap Gris Nez lighthouse as it shone on the bedroom ceiling. I could count twenty between the flashes that spanned the English Channel.

I never remember not being able to swim. Unlike the children of today, we were not allowed to stay in the sea for long periods. One bathe a day, with one extra on very hot days, was the rule, still observed when no adult was with us, though paddling was ad lib.

How we chuckled when a certain woman came down for her early dip. Accompanied by her little maid and fox terrier dog, she daily followed the same routine. The maid relieved her of her towel and wrap: then fastened a rope around her waist. Together they walked down to the sea. The dog sat watching the show.

The dutiful attendant stood back a few yards from the water, holding on to the rope. Never did the ample bathing attire, with its rows and rows of white braid, even get splashed. Waving her arms about, bending up and down, and walking a few yards to the left and to the right in a few inches of water, the daring lady returned to her maid. She took the rope from her mistress's waist and replaced the wrap on her shoulders. Together they walked up the beach to the Parade, followed by the dog. The great adventure was over for another day.

We had a tent, the only one at our end of the beach for many a year. For permission to erect this, my father paid the munificent sum of one shilling a month to the local Council. One day in that tent I learned how an odd remark by an adult can darken a child's world. A happy picnic was in full swing. I was eating a doughnut filled with creamy custard – beastly stuff! Quietly, and as I thought unseen, I scooped out a small hole in the shingle and buried the sticky mess.

Now I could enjoy my doughnut. But no! I heard a friend's voice say: "Now I'll show you something." She uncovered my guilt, and for me the sun went in.

We enjoyed picnics on the lovely sands at Dymchurch, five miles along the coast. In those days, there might be one or two other people about, but more often we had the whole stretch to ourselves. The Romney, Hythe and Dymchurch Railway was not yet. Our own Hythe shore was pebbly with an occasional patch of sand.

Delight reached its climax on bar-sand evenings. These came monthly with the long tide. By late afternoon a bar of sand would begin to appear some way from the shore. The narrow stretch of sea between bar and beach gradually shrank, until it was possible to walk out to the bar. Those of us with long legs got there first.

The fishermen came along with their shrimping nets, and we revelled in searching for small sea creatures and special shells. Late bed was always a privilege on bar-sand nights. At last Mother would come to take me home. I must have been expressing my disappointment at leaving my sisters and older friends behind, for I have never ceased to hear her saying: "There will be other days." Yes, there have been many other days of great happiness, but none so utterly carefree.

Men could undress before six in the morning on the far end of the beach beyond the seawall, where nobody passed by. Apart from this, the byelaws posted at intervals along the Parade seawall forbade any undressing. This rule was strictly enforced, as it was, of course, for women who, unless using a tent, went to and from the beach with wraps over their bathing dresses.

Greatly daring, we would at high tide, when waves dashed up the wall, vie with one another in standing at the edge of the Parade before the next wave broke. Sometimes we were caught and hurried down the road, dripping wet. Mother was indeed patient. "Hurry upstairs and get those wet clothes off" was, as a rule, the extent of her chiding.

My memories of the local school, before I attended one at Folkestone, are very hazy[1]. Ours was a happy family, and I can only think that life at home, school and church – the three focal points – passed pleasantly week after week without any very outstanding happenings.

It is the exceptional event that leaves its mark on a child's conscious memory. I can recall feeling desperately sorry for the children walking away from the Church House[2], where on some winter days there was a free soup kitchen, with a steaming jug of soup in one hand and half a loaf in the other. I used to dread seeing them, and cowardly would take a long walk home from school to avoid passing the Church House. It seemed so unfair. Why should life be so different for some children?

Saturday afternoons were usually set apart for country walks, but, before we started, there would be the weekly pennies to be spent. One day, we looked with astonishment at a big dish amid the jelly-babies, liquorice, marshmallows, pear drops and other good things. It was filled with what looked like dry banana skins, and was labelled 'locust'. We were told that it was what John the Baptist ate (I had always pitied him, thinking he took the big flying insects with his wild honey!).

Awed at being offered something that had been fed to the great prophet, we all had a pennyworth: four ounces. It weighed very light. Cheerfully we left the shop, each of us hugging a big bagful. We made for the country before sampling our treasure. Alas! One taste was enough. We all hated it. With dampened spirits we walked on. Then one of my sisters had a brilliant idea. We often had a

---

[1] Dorothy attended St Leonard's Girls' School, Hythe, 1908 – 1912, and Folkestone County School 1912 – 1917. The St Leonard's Girls' School was part of a school complex opened in 1852, on St Leonard's Road, Hythe, that included an Infants' and a Boys' school. The town was early provided with schools to meet the needs for free education due to the influx of military families from the early 19th Century.

[2] St Leonard's Church House in St Leonard's Road.

paper or chalk chase. "Let's have a locust chase," she called out. We sat in a field and broke the locust into small pieces. Hopefully we tasted it again. But no! Sweets were off for that weekend. The chase was a great success. As we went home, we wondered if the birds would eat the scraps of locust scattered in the lanes and fields.

We knew, and were seldom disappointed, where to find the first white violets, purple orchids and the biggest kingcups growing between the stones in the stream. We thought there were too many gamekeepers about the woods. They did not welcome us, and who can blame them? Our feelings toward them were mixed. We half feared them, and half hoped they would see us and chase us out of the woods.

Jumping the winding streams, even if we sometimes landed in them, was the highlight of country excursions. Normally, we arrived home with somewhat muddy shoes, but one afternoon their state was such that even Mother's patience gave out. So, sadly for a time,

stream jumping was off. Then one of us had a brainwave. Next time we went to the streams we took a paper bag containing a shoe brush and a tin of polish. Before returning home, we sat on the bank cleaning our shoes, and all was well. Stream jumping was on again. Sometimes with a short run and the help of a long pole, we would then take a flying leap.

Dorothy under friendly restraint of twin sisters, Lily (left) and Violet. The teenager seen on the right is brother Arthur Gordon

18. LOCAL PRODUCE

Horse-carts regularly bought products from the Kentish countryside to our door. And local tradesmen used handcarts. As soon as a night's catch was sorted, fishermen would be calling: "Fresh fish, fresh fish." Fresh they certainly were. A little too fresh for my liking, for often an apparently dead plaice would suddenly flap and slither on to the kitchen floor.

The little carts came laden with fruit in season. What a variety! On Saturday, a patrician-like old woman drove in from her farm. Proudly drawing attention to her wares, she never failed to say: "All picked by my own hands last evening." Mother had a standing order with her for half a pound of every kind of fruit she carried: red and white cherries; red, black and white currants; gooseberries, strawberries, raspberries, stone fruits and the rest. Whatever she had went into the traditional large mixed fruit Sunday pie.

When the muffin man announced his arrival, I always hoped that one day, when he turned his head to see if there were any customers behind him, his tray would slip off. It never did, precariously as it swivelled. Suddenly, the 'windmill man' would appear with his handcart gay with wheeling paper windmills on little sticks. As soon as the children saw him, they ran indoors and returned each carrying a two-pound glass jam jar: the price of a windmill. He departed with a cart laden with jars.

On Sunday afternoons, a voice calling 'Watercress, watercress' – actually it said 'watercreases, watercreases' – might be heard. The crier packed his bunches in a large brown wicker basket flung on his back. When Mother heard him she would sometimes say: "I wonder half the town is not dead with typhoid. They've no idea where it comes from."

As Christmas approached, a handcart piled high with little oranges was pushed around the town. It carried the slogan in large letters: "Oh look Mother! Only four a penny." The notice grew grubbier each year. The price remained constant.

Nobody was at home when a large supply of late-keeping pears was delivered to us just before Christmas. They were put in the garden shed. They had not come from a regular trader, nor could we remember the address of the man who supplied them. The following September, Dad and I were cycling along Donkey Street in the Marsh when we passed a farmer in his cart slowly coming along the road. We exchanged greetings and cycled on. Suddenly, however, Dad jumped off his bike, calling out: "That's him." We pedalled back. This was indeed the pear man and, when Dad paid him, he said: "No hurry, Sir. Thank you very much" and went on chewing his straw.

19. "THERE'S A WAR ON"

Long before 1914, we thought of Germany as a 'bogey' over the sea. Occasionally, we would hear: "The Germans are coming." I cannot recall these words having any effect on us at the time. But, subconsciously they must have made their impact, for when a German band came to play near our home, it struck us with terror.

A group of three or four players, with heavy beards, would occasionally take up their stand, with their instruments, on the path. We had to catch but a sight of them before we ran indoors, howling. These bands were the cause of the only real fear I had felt before 1914.

Bank Holiday, August 4th 1914, was a beautiful hot summer day. I was fourteen. My father, who was Secretary[1] at the School of Musketry, told us that we might have to move to Bisley (fortunately we did not). Apart from this, my memory of the warm evening of the day War was declared was of people congregating in small groups. Everywhere you went you met them, and all would be discussing the same question: "What does it mean?"

When I went to the lookout hut to talk to the coastguard on duty, I asked him what it would mean. For the first time I was annoyed with a sailor. He replied: "Enjoy yourself while you can." I was carrying a camera. One who had always spoken in a kindly voice said harshly: "You mustn't bring that thing out again." Adults in whom I had had perfect confidence now could not give an answer when I demanded: "What will it mean?" Suddenly, our sure, free life had ended.

---

[1] Dorothy uses the term Secretary. At Robert Dann's retirement celebration, the Press used the term Steward. The two job titles, at that time, could denote identical responsibilities.

Living on the Kent coast, we were early brought face to face with the realities of war. Regular soldiers were always in the town, taking courses at the School of Musketry [later the Small Arms School]. Activity here soon intensified. Sergeants and other ranks of the Regular Army, who had worked at the School of Musketry and had retired to live in the town, were immediately given commissions. The little town began to fill with Military. I had been going into Folkestone to school for several years. Now, the buses became over-filled with soldiers on the five-mile journey.

Convalescent Homes began to open up. Soon the blue uniforms of the injured mingled with khaki. Often as our bus travelled along the sea road at Sandgate, a troop ship would emerge from the headland on its way to France. Well might World War One be called the singing War. Soldiers were for ever singing as they marched, often accompanied by a band. More and more men came into the district.

The Canadians had large camps up on the hill behind the town. Before long, there were more Canadian soldiers than our own.

Local shops became more prosperous, for the pay of the Canadian men was much higher than that of our Tommies. "We don't fleece you" was cut out in small letters on the blacked-out door or window of many a shop. Unfortunately, this was not always true. As the War advanced, there were soldiers everywhere. Earlier we had thought the town full of Military, but the numbers were nothing compared with what they became; more and more men walked down the hill from the growing camps. Ever-increasing column on column of young men marched along. As the sound of one band died away that of another could be heard further along the ranks.

After school, before catching my bus home, I would sometimes stand and watch the men as they marched endlessly toward what is now known as the Road of Remembrance leading down to the quay, where troop ships were waiting to take them across to France. Day after day it went on. I felt rebellious. Surely someone, somewhere, could bring it to a halt? I knew that in a few days many of these youths, little older than myself, would lie dead on a battlefield. As I watched them, I wondered if their outward cheer reflected their inward feeling.

Helping the Belgian refugees when they landed, often carrying but a small bundle of clothes, had been a salutary experience. We knitted and knitted as if every soldier's life depended on it. In the dinner hour, accompanied by a mistress, we pushed round a barrow to collect newspapers: a minor salvage effort.

One morning, I received a summons to the Head Mistress's room. Our classroom was near. The Head had overhead some of my conversation. After she had given me a lecture, I was told to return to my work. As I was leaving, she said: "Mind you, my dear" – I had never heard the word on her lips before – "I'm not saying that I may not agree with you; but do remember there is a war on." Remember? Could one ever forget it day or night?

We had soldiers billeted on us. One by one they passed to the Front. With tragic regularity, news came through that these kindly men who had shared our home had been killed. Evening after evening Mother would prepare sandwiches for a soldier who had been told to be ready day or night to depart immediately. Then, one morning in the early hours, there was a great knocking at the front door. I did not return to bed, but sat and watched dawn break over the sea. The guns were rumbling over the water. In three days' time this man was killed. One by one they passed to the Front.

20. KITCHENER IS DEAD

One afternoon at school someone came into the form room and spoke to the mistress in charge. I heard the words 'Kitchener,' and 'Town Hall'. Thinking that Kitchener was himself at Folkestone Town Hall, we hurried there as soon as we were released. We found a larger crowd than usual reading the latest War bulletin in the window. It said that Kitchener had been drowned. The bus journey home took half-an-hour.

My father was sitting in the garden, enjoying the lovely weather. I told him the news. He could not believe it. He was a man of gentle speech. The strongest words I ever heard from him, when one of us ignored parental discipline, were: "You silly juggins!" So, when I said: "Kitchener's drowned, Dad," he chuckled and replied: "You silly juggins!"

"He is," I insisted: "the *Hampshire* has been torpedoed off the Orkneys". Without speaking, he went indoors for his hat, then walked into town to see for himself the bulletin in our Town Hall. Little could he, or many others, have foreseen how history would show that the death of the 'Invincible' War Leader brought relief to some politicians.

Unexpectedly, a young officer called and left a notice giving us ten days in which to move from our house. The open land at the back being suitable for a kite-balloon station, so nearby houses were being requisitioned. Every available property in the town had been claimed by the Military. A house built for Sir Charles Wakefield was completed just in time for the soldiers to move in. Its beautiful fireplaces were protected by wood panelling. Alas! The big nails were hammered through the wood into the fireplaces. On the ninth day we had no idea where we were going. There just was no accommodation.

Then, owing to a sudden death, we were offered a house if we would ask the Military to wait a few more days. Miracles might still happen, but not that one. The owners of the house, however, agreed to leave their furniture on one side of the rooms and for ours to go to the other side, until they could make their own arrangements.

So on the tenth day we moved in. For a time the muddle was unbelievable. This was accepted stoically by older family members as being part of the necessary price of war. For myself, I had never moved before and thoroughly enjoyed the novelty.

Eventually, we settled down. One evening, Dad and I walked past the old home and spoke to a soldier standing at the gate. He had been a gardener before enlisting and had been pleased to find a grape vine in the little greenhouse at the bottom of the garden. When the soldiers departed after the War, we found everything wooden had been used for firing. The only bright spot was the grape vine. This was in very good heart.

The day we returned home, I complained about the taste of the water. The tank in a cupboard in the room at the top of the house was heaped with bones. This room, the biggest in the house, was used by the men for their meals. All bones had been thrown into the tank. The decorators had not thought of opening the tank cupboard. We marvelled that the men had not been poisoned: perhaps they had used water from one of the neighbouring houses.

21. CATCHING SPIES

I sometimes went for a walk along the lonely beach toward Dymchurch. Away from the road or Parade, this part of the shore, with Romney Marsh stretching behind – though open to all – was seldom used. I never met anyone there. So, when I reached the remains of a Martello Tower and climbed on to a part of the fallen wall, I was startled to see a man and woman behind it. They were sitting close together, with a map spread over their laps. The wind and the sea pounding on the stones had silenced my footsteps.

The strangers, ejaculating in German, were as astonished to see me jumping down from the high rock, as I was to see them. Using perfect English, they questioned me. Being scared, I wanted to race back along the beach but stayed talking awhile, explaining that I often came this way as my home was very near.

"Where are you going now?" the man asked as I began to climb up the rock. "Home to my dinner," I replied: "the tide will be up before long." I walked back along the shore, fighting my way against the wind and not a little scared. I had only one thought. I must go and tell Mr Harvey.

When I got back to the Parade, I went to the lookout hut. The Chief Officer, Mr Harvey, was on duty. "You're back soon," he said. I sat on his wooden bench and told him what I had seen. "Had the woman a red beret?" he asked. "They went along some time ago. I was surprised at anyone going along in this wind." And he added: "I know no weather stops you, but everyone's not so crazy!"

We waited and waited for the man and woman to return along the beach, their only way back. The tide was coming in, however, and we knew we should not have to wait much longer. The Chief Officer constantly used his spyglass and at last called out: "They're coming." He let them reach the Parade and walk some distance

In the early years of the 20th Century, Hythe seafront facing west. Note the line of Martello Towers, starting with Tower number 13 near the beach end of St Leonard's Road (as shown on map on pages 64/65)

down the road before coming out of his hut and following them. I was told to keep a good way behind. As I passed home, I ran in and a sister joined me. We followed them until we were some distance along the Dymchurch Road running parallel to the beach where the couple had been sitting.

The Chief Officer then caught up with them. They took papers out of their bag and handed them to him. He had a quick look at them. As soon as the three of them turned round and began walking back, my sister and I hurried into a side road. We let them get well ahead before following them. We had no idea where they were going but kept a discreet distance. They entered the Police Station.

Later in the day, I went to the lookout hut to see the Chief Officer who would say nothing except: "You ought to be feeling pleased with yourself." Several days later, the newspapers reported that two spies – a man and a woman – had paid the price at the Tower of London. I took a newspaper to the lookout hut and again tried to get the CO to tell me what he knew. Again, all he would say was: "I told you, you should be very pleased with yourself."

It all happened over half-a-century ago. Were the executed man and woman the ones I had startled by jumping down from the ruined Martello Tower? With mixed feelings, I have never ceased to wonder[1].

Every house received an official form telling us what to do in the event of an invasion. We were to proceed towards West Hythe along the canal bank – the Royal Military Canal – built at the same time as the Martello Towers along the coast as a defence against Napoleon. We never knew, and shall never know, what the programme was to be on our reaching West Hythe. Our luggage was to be restricted to one small parcel. We were much amused by two elderly ladies, always immaculately dressed with 'leg of mutton' sleeves, who let us know that their parcels would contain their best white silk blouses.

When moonlight nights brought over the raiders, some townsfolk sought safety in a Martello Tower that stood near us. Much as we dreaded the raids, we looked forward to the evening trek of people passing our home on their way to the Tower. The two immaculate ladies, one pushing the other in a bath chair, brought their parcels: they would never be parted from their best white silk blouses. It was sometimes an eye-opener to see what was most prized by men and women one had known for many years.

---

[1] This account of meeting the spies was found as a separate article and I used it in preference to the description of the same event in Dorothy's main MS because it is a little more detailed and mentions the Chief Officer's name.

Of course there were no sirens to warn us of air raids. Large black cones were hoisted at strategic places. When the coastguards received the 'All Clear' the CO would walk down the road calling out 'All Clear, All Clear.' He sometimes woke us up when we had been unaware that enemy planes had been over.

Soldiers packed the churches. For our own Methodist[2] service on Sunday evening, chairs had always to be placed in the aisles, while the pulpit steps provided more seats. The men asked if from six o'clock to six-thirty, when normal worship began, they could sing hymns from the Sankey collection. And how they sang! Unfortunately, the building would not hold nearly all who would have liked to be there.

One Sunday, it was as if a magic broom had swept the roads completely free of men in uniform – not one soldier was in church. Wild rumours circulated. It transpired that the authorities had wanted to test how quickly all troops could be recalled to camp. I think we were more alarmed on that Sunday evening than on any other occasion during the War.

---

2   Hythe Wesleyan Methodist Church on Rampart Road was opened in 1898.

22. FOOD SHORTAGES

How blest we were – little as we realized it at the time – who were young with healthy digestions, compared with some of the elderly and sick. The type of food available toward the end of the War must have been a sore trial to many. Pale yellow maize flour was used for cakes. The dark coarse bread became the only kind available. Cards with EAT LESS BREAD were delivered to every house to be displayed in windows.

One dinner hour at school, a mistress asked two of us if we would like to go into town with her. She had heard that one of the shops – a rare occasion – was selling butter. Margarine was the order of the day. What dreadful stuff it was: we called it cart grease. Butter was not rationed. The supply was insufficient to make rationing practicable. The more eagerly was it sought when news went round that this or that shop had a small amount.

There was a long queue outside the shop. Each person was allowed two ounces: little enough, but riches then. It was an extra hot day. As we walked back to school, I was wondering whether it would be better to keep the precious butter in my desk or shoe locker. When we reached the school gates, the mistress told us to come in with her. Holy of holies, we had never before entered by the front door! Telling us to wait in the hall, she went to her study, returning with the exact money for our butter. Without speaking, she handed this to us and took our butter. She walked away saying: "Hurry to the cloakroom to get ready for afternoon school."

Speechless, we did as we were told. But once we got there our tongues were loosed. A young mistress on duty stopped us for making so much noise and added: "And you, sixth formers." We gave her our story. "Poor dears," she said. Poor indeed! It would be many a long week before we would see butter again. Schoolgirls may then have been more docile than they are now; but, as the story circulated, that mistress, forfeiting respect of pupils and staff, paid dearly for her extra tea-time treat.

I still remember our bliss – not too strong a word – on a winter's night when a number of us were going to choir practice. (We never went out alone late. Looking back, I can record that, with the town and district so full of troops, I never heard of one unpleasant incident.)

We met a member of our church who told us to go to his own nearby greengrocer's shop, where unexpectedly a big block of dates had been delivered. We were allowed two pounds each of those squashy dates. In later years, the choicest of chocolates have never tasted so good. To us starved of sweets for many a month, their nectar was intoxicating. Not even an irate choirmaster, who 'couldn't understand what was going on', could check our devouring them.

Our school [Folkestone County School] had been damaged in one of the earliest daylight raids. Unhappily, the caretaker was there and was killed. Otherwise, as it was the beginning of the half-term holiday, no-one else was about. The school was partly re-opened at the time of the harvest moon, and the nights were much disturbed. The hymn chosen for prayer on the opening day included the lines:

And the silver moon by night
Shining with her gentle light.

My eyes caught those of the Latin mistress standing near. We both suppressed a smile. The silver moon hadn't given us much cause to sing her praise the last few nights.

23. SOLDIERS REMEMBERED

As time went on, we had come to regard the troops as part of normal life. There were far more blue uniforms of the wounded to be seen. These added a little cheer, for – due to the terrible losses on the battlefield – so many people were now in mourning, which was then seldom anything but black. For many weeks, a number of Belgian soldiers travelled on our morning bus. They were always keen to see our homework and schoolbooks, largely, I think, because in us they saw their own children. As we rode along by the sea, they would point across the water, with remarks such as: "Marie Jose will be going to school over there."

The Star and Garter Home[1] had a branch in Sandgate. A donkey would stand at the gate, ready to pull an invalid carriage up the hill to Folkestone. The climb was too steep for the men to manage the hand-propelled carriages on their own. At the top the donkey was released. Then it would enter another gate and walk by itself through the Home's grounds to the bottom of the hill, there to await the next invalid carriage needing its help.

Due to Canadian troops being stationed in the district we saw the unfolding of a family saga that, once more, proved truth to be stranger than fiction. Parents living in a small cottage with their children decided to emigrate to Canada. Their father went in advance to find work and to prepare a home. That was the end of any communication with his family until one day, the eldest child, a

---

[1] The Royal Star and Garter Home was established as an independent Charity in 1916 to care for severely disabled young men returning from the battlegrounds of the First World War. Old hotel premises on Richmond Hill were quickly found to be impracticable and were pulled down and replaced with a purpose-built home. Residents were moved to temporary accommodation, which the Royal Star and Garter owned at Sandgate. Today, the Royal Star and Garter Home at Richmond Hill continues to offer care and rehabilitation to disabled ex-Service people.

young girl when her father left, was now about to be married. He stood at the bottom of a narrow passage that led up to the cottage. He asked a passing child if Mrs ... still lived there. Being told that she did, he asked the child to go up and tell her that a soldier wished to speak to her. She walked down the passage, and faced her husband. They joined up again, the family rejoicing in owning a father. At the end of the war, all departed happily together for Canada.

An abiding memory of these years is of a Welsh company who, meeting every night for a roll-call a few yards from our house, would – weather permitting – stay on singing for a considerable time. Previously, I had never heard such singing.

My most poignant memory is that of the young soldiers' feet forever marching along our roads. After more than half-a-century there are times when their tramp, tramp, tramp still haunts me.

Folkestone 1914 – 1918[2]

The air is vibrant with the sound
Left in the wake of history.
How many trod this ground
Down to the quay?
How many walked that road no more?
Spirits alone came home
To linger near the shore.
Freely they roam,
Treading this hallowed way.
Still, still I hear the rhythmic beat
Reverberating day by day
Of marching feet.

---

2 This poem by Dorothy K Thomas was published but I do not know where or exactly when because the newspaper/magazine name and date is cut off from the news cutting.

The Star and Garter Home at Sandgate (shown left). The men in the hand-propelled wheelchairs would each be pulled up the hill by a donkey as Dorothy describes. A closer view of the type of wheelchair is shown in the second photo, from the Star and Garter archives, of a wounded soldier tending chickens at the Sandgate Home

Dad was Honorary Secretary of the Soldiers' and Sailors' Association. He would sometimes come home in the afternoon for a short rest. Too often, this would be disturbed by a soldier's wife or widow seeking advice. They should have gone elsewhere at appointed times, but they knew they would get a sympathetic hearing from Dad. I greatly admired his never-failing patience and courtesy toward them.

One woman was distressed because, in all innocence, she had received an allowance for her child beyond the allotted time, and with her small means she could not repay the excess. I chuckled at a story told by a member of the SSA Committee. When this woman's case was brought up, Lady … asked: "Does she attend church?" Dad immediately answered: "My dear Lady, we are not here to discuss this woman's religion but her pressing need."

When a soldier was killed in action, his widow could have a pension or take a lump sum of money. With so many troops in the town, no woman, unless she wished, need remain a widow. It was no uncommon thing for a woman, during the course of the War, to receive two or three lump sums. One day, Dad came from interviewing a widow who had called at the house. "She's done it again," he said. "Wouldn't hear of a pension, so that's her fourth lump sum."

One consequence of the greater gulf between the sexes was that during the War, there was no compulsory service for women. Many volunteered for nursing. As the need for female labour in industry especially in the munitions factories became urgent, high wages were used as indispensable bait. The trade unions, with whom the Government could not afford to quarrel, successfully maintained their policy of 'no Industrial Conscription' throughout the War. Reluctantly, with some dissentients, they agreed to the Military Service Act of 1916.

This was the first time that large numbers of untrained women had earned good money in their own right, and the repercussions have continued ever since.

24. TEACHING BECKONS

As some of we girls neared the age of eighteen and daily saw the casualty lists growing longer and longer, we were brought face to face with the fact that – had we been boys – we should in all probability never have a career. From an early age I had been constant in my desire to teach. I was sorry for some of my friends who had no wish to teach or to nurse. The possibility of other careers for women was seldom discussed. If an unorthodox suggestion was made, there too often came the reply: "That's a man's job." In 1917, a small secretarial class was started at school. This inspired more ambitious girls, who wanted something beyond 'shorthand-typing', to envisage a career as a private secretary.

Some psychologists say it is unhealthy for pupils to have too great a liking for a schoolmaster or mistress. Be that as it may, I would have endured much for several of my mistresses. I still think of them with gratitude and affection. There must have been the best type of discipline, since we were never unduly conscious of it. The staff did not arrive in the form rooms at the last minute. They were there a good while before prayers, during which time we moved about and talked freely. Some knowledge and ideas thus gained have remained more vital than much taught formally.

I have lived to bless our English mistress, who did not set any particular poem for homework but left us to make our own choice from *The Golden Treasury*. The result was a store of poems learnt by heart, and still – in advancing years – remembered[1].

One morning, our far-sighted Geography mistress entered the classroom, dumped her books on the desk, and then confronting us

---

[1] Dorothy even in high age, and finally when very ill, would still happily remember a wide selection of long and short poems thus memorised. She would discuss ideas they raised.

resolutely yet with a kindly smile said: "Now, before we begin our lesson, I want to mention something I have been thinking about. Remember this: as a child grows up, the mother must gradually release her hold." I wondered what on earth was coming! She went on to tell us that she saw very plainly how England, as the Mother Country, would not be able indefinitely to maintain top place in the world.

Countries within the Empire – and the United States – would come to surpass us. "I shan't see it," she added. "But I think you will." She insisted that there was no cause for alarm or depression in what, to her mind, should be accepted as a natural process. How right she was!

Dorothy, Pupil Teacher, aged sixteen

Before being accepted as a teacher, one had to pass a medical examination. With a friend who also hoped to become a teacher, I had to travel to Canterbury for this purpose. "Is there any insanity in the family?" the woman doctor asked as I entered the room. Before I could answer, I was asked if I had ever had any goitre trouble! My startled look brought forth: "Don't worry, Rossetti always painted his beauties with full necks." That was the beginning and end of the test. I had passed my 'medical'!

I walked out of the room, full neck and all: an abnormality never noted before or since. My first encounter with educational procedure was over! For good or ill, I was set upon the road to educate the young of England.

We wanted to get home before the moon, now nearly full, was up. Almost certainly the raiders would be visiting us. We left the train at Sandling Junction – that delightful little station – and walked along the country road down the hill. Many soldiers were on their way back to camp. "Good night, sister. Good night, sister," the Canadian voices continually called out.

Already the searchlights were playing, their long arms stretching across the sea. My friend and I parted, hurrying to our homes just as the guns at Dover gave warning of approaching Jerries. I took to my heels along our road, and for the first time, after he had taken up duty by the letter-box months ago, forgot the sentry on duty. He yelled: "Halt" as I ran past. Turning, I saw the moon shining on his fixed bayonet. I gave the usual reply, and needed no encouragement to obey his: "Advance, friend. All's well."

I became a Pupil Teacher: the name given to students, once accepted, before they entered training college. You became attached to a school where you would begin to get some teaching practice.

Miss D. R. Dann has served her apprenticeship with much credit. — She has shown much ability in the management of her classes, Is kind & sympathetic but has a strong will. — Her lessons have been well & carefully prepared. and she possesses originality. — She is hard working, conscientious & capable — She is a good disciplinarian.

Head Teacher of Day School.

Storace. L.L.A —

July 31. 19·8

Dorothy's testimonial of being a Pupil Teacher at Hythe [Council] Girls' School for entry to Southlands Training College

During this time, one day a week was spent at your own school. I found this very enjoyable, though it did seem to be a somewhat haphazard arrangement. The day was Tuesday: why I do not know. You joined in the usual lessons on the time-table for that day. You might be fortunate in that your chosen subjects were on that day, or you might have to drop them until you went to college.

Very lucky were those girls attached to a school whose Headmistress saw they had plenty of practice: though they may not have thought so at the time. The school where I was to begin my teaching – for four days a week – had, for some time, been one short on the staff. So, for my first day, I was put in front of a class and left[1].

Sometimes, in the early days, one could have wished oneself in any other place. I have never forgotten a student who, years later, came to my then class to give her first lesson. It was Scripture, the first lesson of the day. The Headmistress told her to say the Lord's Prayer with the children. She said a few sentences and stopped short. She turned away from the class with a troubled face. "Begin again," said the Mistress. Once more the novice tried and faltered. "Begin again!" Another try, and this time all was well. Those early lessons were a nightmare: it was amazing how suddenly blank the mind could become!

It was interesting to watch the faces of small children when a raw recruit stood in front of them. An electric current seemed to run round the class, stirring the liveliest to rebellion! Unless the teacher commanded attention from the outset, the whole class became restless. There was nothing like knowing the names of some of the children. A boy began to play up. If – correctly – you called him by his name, a look of puzzlement would pass over his face. You could see him thinking: "Coo! She knows me." The first round was won!

---

1 Dorothy was a pupil teacher four days a week 1916 – 1918 at Hythe [Council] Girls' School. One day a week she continued at her own school, Folkestone County School, and she was awarded a P. E.C: an examination which qualified her to enter teachers' training college.

It is unrealistic to expect that everyone who enters the teaching world does so for a vocation. The sheer numbers required every year make this impossible. Whatever other pros and cons there may be, I would advise nobody to choose teaching as a career unless he or she is happy in the company of children. Heaven help them otherwise!

Fifty years ago the classrooms were quieter than they are today. This does not necessarily mean that the children were suppressed. Youngsters were expected to be quiet during lesson time, though I used to allow talking during Handwork periods, not always with the full approval of older members of the staff. 'Steam' was certainly let off in the playground for fifteen or twenty minutes morning and afternoon and, weather permitting, physical exercises were taken outside. It is good that there is now less rigidity, but it riles me when I hear it suggested as a generalization that children fifty years ago were cribbed and confined. In my experience, they were normally eager to get to school and enjoyed life there with their teachers. There were, of course, exceptions, but I can only testify that the atmosphere of the schools in which I taught was happy.

I only knew one boy in three schools (in very different districts) in which I taught for nine years being 'un-teachable'. He had a lovely face, always benign and smiling. The letters in a reading book remained for him mere marks on a page – nothing more. But even he had his day of glory. His father and grandfather kept the donkeys on the beach. From the time this lad could trot along with the donkeys, he had taken the money for the rides. He staggered the class, no less than the teacher, on the day when we began to talk of money sums. His face beamed with light of the knowledge that in his field at least was his.

But this is looking too far forward. I worked very hard preparing lessons and teaching four days a week. I cannot say the same about the day-a-week spent at my old school. It was good to meet friends and members of staff week after week. Those of us who spent these odd days in this way thoroughly enjoyed them, but we felt they could have been spent more profitably.

On the other hand, the Headmistress of the Infants' School where I was teaching made up my syllabus for the coming week. She certainly did not mean me to be idle! All went well with my work in the classroom except for Scripture. From the outset of my teaching, I felt that all was not well with the way in which Scripture – now Religious Instruction – was taught. The Head was a happy, sensible woman, fully alert to the needs of the children and friendly and helpful to the staff. She was sympathetic and imaginative in her approach to all subjects except Scripture, about which she would not admit discussion.

I always looked for the coming week's programme for Scripture with apprehension. I struggled on until I saw that the syllabus for the next fortnight was on angels. This involved ten periods. There was a list of their visitations from the Old and New Testament. The first lesson was to be a description of an angel's appearance and work. No! I just couldn't do it, and with trepidation I told the Head so. "I am surprised," she said. "I did not think you were irreligious. Teach them, then, the set hymn." This was:

Around the throne of God a band
Of glorious angels ever stand.

Not perhaps the best choice of a hymn for six-year olds! But I did my best. How poor a best was soon to be shown.

The children had large sheets of drawing paper and their own pastels. All were free to make pictures of any story or of anything else they liked. While they were busy, I walked round the room looking at their efforts. Most modern children may be more skilful at actual drawing, but it seems to me that finished pictures are not so individual. I could be sure that every effort, if not always very good, would at least be the child's own creation. Often today, children's pictures reflect standardizing influences, even though the total effect is clever. Modern life and education leave a child all too little time for imagination, for daydreaming, for floating away into a world of his own.

I sat in the small desk by a girl and looked and looked at what she had drawn. "You tell me about it" I said. "You know, Miss, around the throne of God." Then I understood. There was God in the middle of the page, high on a stool, with a huge yellow crown on his head. All over the page were men playing instruments – one a drum, one a fiddle, several blowing what I took to be various kinds of horns or trumpets: all had crowns, all had enormous white wings. A glorious band indeed around the throne of God! No, my Scripture teaching hadn't been very successful, much as it may have brought forth a work of art.

The school, built about 1910, was well-planned, light and cheerful to work in. The five classrooms opened on to the central hall. The Head had no room of her own. Her desk stood between two entrances – no doors – that led from the hall to the cloakroom. Classrooms were heated by huge coal fires, but there was no heat in the hall. The Head must have found it chilly and draughty. Yet I never heard any complaint. The staff had to hang their coats in a mere passageway, with a washbasin and lavatory at the end. And, at the time, this school was deemed 'modern'. In fairness, however, I must reiterate that there was never any grumbling about the amenities, or lack of them. The Head spent much of her time going round the classes. Later, in this sized school, the Head had a class of her own, while Heads in the larger schools had to teach for a stated number of hours.

Pupil teachers had an allowance for books. The small monthly cheque came with the staff's salary from the Kent Education Committee. I do not know if all Education Committees gave this grant.

War had brought its sorrows but also its excitements. By 1918, little of the latter remained. Air raids had ceased. We had no fear of them restarting. For so long we had heard that the Germans were crumbling, yet the misery of it all dragged on. A child – too young to understand the full tragedy – would sometimes come up and say: "My daddy's killed, teacher." It seemed so unfair that friends with several sons should one by one hear of their deaths, while we – all girls in the family – were left unscathed. At long last, it became plain that the War was nearing its end.

By this time variety in food was indeed limited. Vegetables were very scarce. I came home from town one morning carrying with great pride a large Swede turnip. Its normal cost would have been about a halfpenny. I had paid nine pence. My mother became very adept in cutting in half our rare eggs. Cooking them until well set, she would get two eggcups and, with one swift sure stroke of the knife, would cut an egg in half and would deftly pop the halves into two eggcups. Her skill never let her down.

How we young folk longed for sweets! I could never understand why a small shop some distance out of the town should suddenly have a small allowance of them. The news quickly spread and our young legs took us in record time to the shop. One such occasion took my friend and me to a tiny shop high up the hill near the old Church. We took our chocolate creams into the churchyard and ate them as we walked around. Standing by the grave[1] of Lionel Lukin, the inventor of the lifeboat, we talked about the coming months that would find us at training college.

The four years of war had necessarily restricted people's movements. The young stayed at home. Apart from holidays with relatives in London's suburbia in my early teens, I had no experience of town life. I had never met anyone who had been to a teachers training college. So little did we fear any further trouble from the War, that there was not the slightest apprehension at beginning life in a London training college[2] on October 1st 1918.

---

1 In St Leonard's churchyard, Hythe.
2 Southlands College, Battersea.

27. SOUTHLANDS TRAINING COLLEGE

I went prepared to enjoy myself, never doubting that the College[1] would be in a good open district. Disillusionment came all too soon. The taxi passed through an inner South Western suburb and drew up at the big College gate. My heart sank. By no effort of imagination could the area be described as other than semi-slummy. My thoughts were on retreat: on returning home. I wasn't prepared for this! I pulled myself together, gave an extra good tip for luck, and opened the gate.

What a transformation! I was in a pleasant garden, with a building standing some way back. It was said that this building had originally been a convent. Part of the grounds, in which some of the older tutors remembered rabbits running around, were now covered by lecture rooms, hall and a new wing. A large garden and lawn remained, good to sit or walk in except when the wind wafted the smell from Price's candle factory.

The majority of the students were housed in dormitories specially built for the purpose, others in the old building, where the large rooms were divided. These latter accommodated those of us whose names, on an alphabetical basis, came early. How much in life can sometimes depend on that first letter of your surname! I was horrified when I saw one of these divided rooms, but could have cried aloud for joy that my own part of it had a window opening on to a balcony.

---

[1] Southlands College Archives have Dorothy's College records at the time of her entry. They show that her health was 'A1'. The Head Teacher of Folkestone County School, which Dorothy attended from age twelve, described her as "Average ability. Gives evidence of becoming a good teacher. Pleasing manner, kind and sympathetic. Good tempered. Painstaking." The Methodist Minister of the Wesleyan Methodist Church in Hythe said she was a Sunday school and Band of Hope worker of 'excellent character'.

On the left is a side-gate on High Street, Battersea, into Southlands College. It is not the big College gate Dorothy refers to. The scene in the High Street is similar to the one that greeted Dorothy. Part of the College is shown behind the side-gate. The taller building on the left is Southlands Infants' School, a teaching school attached to the College. From Southlands College Archives, University of Surrey Roehampton

There were five divisions, three of which had no windows. The wooden partitions nearly reached the ceiling, shutting out so much of the daylight that electric light was often needed[2]. That any student in the 20th Century – in a College of quite high repute – should have to spend so much time in these small dark rooms, airless unless the girls with the windows chose to open them, struck me at the time as wrong and now, in retrospect, seems incredible. I received so much gratitude, quite undeserved, from the girl next

---

2   In post-War improvements to the College: '. . . cubicles were altered so as to do away with some that had no windows' [from *Retrospect – Prospect 1872 – 1928. Southlands Training College, Battersea, SW*]. Student fees in 1918 were £17 10s.

Front view of Southlands College during Dorothy's time. It is easy to see which was the original house with extensions each side added at different times

South view of Southlands College overlooking the large garden. Both photos from the publication Retrospect – Prospect 1872 - 1928, Southlands Training College, Battersea. From Southlands College Archives, University of Surrey Roehampton

door to me, who came from Westmorland, for letting in so much air. In our second year, we moved into the new wing. The College, under the auspices of the Methodist Church, moved years ago to a more salubrious neighbourhood.

Some students were markedly unsophisticated at the start. How rapidly, as they experienced a broadening life, some of them changed! One afternoon, a few of us were going to Oxford Street. A shy girl came up to me and asked if she could join us. A number of times she did not merely ask if she could keep with me; she implored me not to leave her. She stuck to me like a limpet, often holding on to my arm. Until journeying to College, she had never been in a train.

Suddenly, in Selfridges, I exclaimed: "Where is she?" We had lost her. I remembered that she had been with us in the lift, so to the lift we returned, and waited for its descent. There she was going up and down, up and down. "I knew you would come back for me," she said with an innocent smile. Within a month or two, she was finding her way round with the best, putting us all in the shade. Was there ever a quicker metamorphosis? I tried to picture the faces of her relatives and friends when she returned to the West Country after her first term.

There were lectures in the morning and evening. Afternoons were free. The recently appointed Principal[3] had been Head of a girls' boarding school. Some felt she had not made the adjustment. We saw little of her: she did not mix with the students. There were 150 of us, mostly between the ages of eighteen and twenty. Several were older. Looking back on those days, I find it remarkable, though memory confirms the fact, that the majority of us were not even inwardly conscious of the urge to revolt. No such idea entered our conversation. The pendulum always swings too far and, if today, it is overbalanced in one direction, it was certainly so in the opposite direction fifty years ago. If students are now too ready to complain,

---

3   Miss C E Brunyate MA.

we were perhaps too docile. We ought to have rebelled against some conditions, including some sanitary ones, and restrictions unwarranted for students who were no longer children.

No girl was ever allowed to go out of College alone. In fairness, it must be said that it was not then the done thing for young women to walk alone about London. But we could never go anywhere. I sometimes longed to get away from everything and roam about on my own. If we wanted to meet a friend outside the College we had to apply to the Principal for permission. The appointed time was after our breakfast.

She sat alone in her room, with her breakfast before her. How good the thickly buttered toast looked as her fingers toyed with it! One of my sisters [Maud] was a nursing sister in the base hospital at Etaples. My only chance of seeing her before she returned to France from leave was to catch an earlier train than the one I normally travelled by when I went home at half-term. I should have missed no lecture. I had to queue up with other girls seeking permission for this or that. My request was turned down. I was nineteen at the time!

The student standing next to me in the queue was hoping she could leave College in time to see her brother before he returned to the Front. But no! She could not. When she returned to College, wearing black for the brother she never saw again, I wondered if the Principal had any qualms.

28. TEACHING PRACTICE

Six weeks was, I believe, the minimum time then prescribed by the Board of Education for a student at a training college to give to teaching, or – as it was called – school practice, during her two-year course. Our College increased those weeks considerably, I think to twelve. This did not mean that the whole time was spent in teaching.

Usually, two students went together to a chosen school. They spent all of the time in the classroom, but taught only the appointed lessons. If any of us wanted to change from senior to junior school or vice versa, opportunity was given to try this in a practical way. Some students thus discovered, what they might never otherwise have done, the age group for which they were best fitted.

At certain times, a large number of students went on teaching practice. This meant visits to many schools. Some were near, but others involved considerable journeys. One was next door to the College[1]. I was standing in its playground one morning when a tutor came to speak to me. "You see that girl, and that bigger one there, and that boy?" They all looked strange. "There are several younger ones and two in the big school. The mother came here as a child: should have been sterilized." She spoke with passionate concern, then walked away, leaving me mystified, since the word 'sterilized' conveyed nothing to me. After supper, I went into the Library and became more enlightened. Today those children would be in a special school.

I thoroughly enjoyed my experience in the different schools. The buildings might sometimes be dismal. What flights of steps we often mounted! But the children, for the most part, were cheerful. How I 'fell' for the Cockney youngsters – so alert and out for fun –

---

1   This was, in fact, Southlands Infants' School, run by the College. Dorothy did teaching practice there June 30th – July 11th and September 17th – September 30th 1919.

Dann family photo taken in 1918. Back row left to right: Lily, Maud, father Robert, Emmeline and Violet. Front row left to right: Dorothy, Daisy with daughter Barbara, mother Martha and May. My cousin Edna found this gem among her photos. It is the only photo I have seen with the seven adult sisters all together

when first I taught them. I asked if I could do some teaching in a slum area. In one extra gloomy school[2], where the children were poorly clad – it was always footwear that first betrayed poverty – I came near to trouble.

I entered the playground alone. A crowd of senior boys pelted me with carrots: they must have brought them for a Nature lesson. I was scared. Those boys, the eldest not more than fourteen, seemed huge as they came nearer, taking aim. I picked up a carrot that, after hitting me, had dropped at my feet. I threw it sky-high; fortunately I could throw with the best. The boys cheered and clapped and followed suit: but my throws outdid them all.

Meanwhile, I was walking to the Infants' entrance. With what relief, despite the now-changed spirit of the boys, I reached it. The victory, however, was complete. Every day, while I remained at that school, the boys met me at the gate and grinning hailed me as 'Carrots'.

Visits to schools were not without light relief. The Head of one Infant Department came in a big car: a rare sight in those days. Her husband was a Bank Manager. In Kent, women teachers had to retire at marriage. This was the first time I realized that this rule did not extend everywhere. She was short, fat, and fussily dressed. When all were assembled in the hall for morning prayers, she sailed in and stood on a little platform facing the school. There she waited for utter silence. Then, wagging her head, rolling her eyes and keeping time with a much be-ringed hand she sang:

Good morning to you,
Good morning to you,
Good morning, dear children,
Good morning to you.

---

2 Dorothy did teaching practice at Battersea Park Road Infants' School January 13th – February 10th 1920. Her College records state: "Miss Dann is a promising teacher. Alert, capable, takes pains over work. Introduction of group work into large class is difficult, yet was creditably managed. Should prove progressive and become valuable teacher."

One boy, near to whom I stood daily for a week, added under his breath: "The same to you, with knobs on it." I hadn't the heart to chide him.

That a tutor might suddenly walk into a classroom while you were teaching did not add to a student's composure. I was grateful to the Headmistress who had left me in front of a class for weeks on end when I was a pupil teacher. Though jittery if I had to speak to adults, nerves vanished in front of children. Some students had done no teaching, others only a little. A student could leave college after passing the final examination at the end of the then two-year course, as a fully qualified teacher, even though she had done the minimum of actual teaching. Good – perhaps brilliant – she might have been on paper, but this was of small avail when she confronted a big, lively class. The only way in which to prove yourself to be a good teacher is to teach and teach and teach.

Was it to be wondered at that some un-certificated teachers – there were then a large number of them – viewed with mixed feelings these young beginners straight from college? Since her cheque was so much smaller at the end of the month, the un-certificated teacher needed something of the grace of God when summoned, as she sometimes was, to restore order in a rebellious class which the college trained novice could no longer control. Some of these older women may have been relatively poor teachers, but I met a number of them in different schools and admired their work and, above all, their love and concern for the children.

When at last the decree went forth that there were no longer to be un-certificated teachers, I rejoiced in the equal status now granted to those who had given so many years' devoted but ill-paid service. Henceforth the only avenue to teaching was through a training college, though – due to exceptional circumstances after World War Two – this rule was temporarily waived.

Some college girls who had done little or no teaching now had to stand in front of a strange class, with the teacher in the room, and with the ever-present fear that a tutor might appear through the door to inspect and to criticise. Back in college, the student would take her book to the tutor, with the comments on her teaching that the latter had written in. Weaknesses would be pointed out and helpful suggestions given. Some students dreaded these interviews.

Tutors' remarks in the classrooms were sometimes unexpected. I had planned a big model of a Red Indian village. Every boy and girl was busy making something for it. A group were sticking odd bits of fur on small dolls that they had already painted a swarthy colour. A tutor walked in and went straight up to these children. She exclaimed loudly: "I wish I could stick fur on a man." My fellow student burst out laughing, but quickly disguised her mirth as coughing and hastened out of the room. The tutor suggested that I should go after her as she was 'choking rather badly'.

Controlling ourselves, we returned, but nearly had to retreat again when we saw this tiny middle-aged woman with curls falling over her forehead, holding up a small doll, very well covered, for all the class to see and joyfully calling out: "There! I have stuck fur on a man." I was sorry for those students to whom school practice was so much of an ordeal that they could not fully enjoy the rich incidental fun that accompanied the hard work.

Some of us made day visits to special schools: for the mentally deficient, the deaf, and the blind. I have never forgotten the face of a young girl in a school for defective speech. As we entered the room, a number of children were enacting a scene from *Peter Pan*. A woman teacher was helping them to say odd words. When Peter appeared, this girl – about eight-years old – said: "Peter Pan" slowly but with perfect enunciation except for her silent 't' in Peter. Her face glowed with the joy of accomplishment.

I wonder if Margaret and Rachel Mcmillan[3] had any inkling of how their ideas, put to practical use in their own nursery school in East London would bear fruit? Toddlers, poorly clad, were left at the school while their mothers went out to work. The children were delighted to change into overalls, kept for their use at school. With their sandpits, toys and classrooms open to the air, they spent hours of happiness in this oasis in a dreary district. Somewhat untidy in long black dresses, the pioneer sisters gave little thought to their own clothes.

---

[3] Margaret and Rachel McMillan were best known for the Open Air Nursery Movement which they founded, first in Bradford, then London. Their ideas spread and, after the 1905 Education Act, nursery schools spread across the country.

29. WAR ENDS

When the guns proclaimed the Armistice, some of us were in the gymnasium. Occasionally, the Gym tutor would hand over the class to a student. It is surprising what commands can be given in Gym – or any other lesson – by a somewhat nervous beginner. The rule was to do just what we were told: however strange the command, you carried it out. Once a student, in a loud confident voice, called out: "Feet up" instead of "Arms up." Some obeyed by doing handstands, others lay flat raising their feet high into the air. The teacher, unaware of her mistake, looked mystified.

The student in charge at 11 o'clock on November 11th 1918 was just about to give the command: "Hips firm" when the guns went off. It was: "Hip hurrah" that resounded through the Gym. All cheered lustily. Matron, acting quickly, had a scratch meal prepared, so that we could all get up to Town and join in the celebrations. What a day of utter abandonment! How did the people hang on to the buses, sitting astride over the sides of the then open upper decks? Did ever men keep calmer under difficulties than London's bus drivers and conductors that afternoon? Cockney wit abounded. I doubt if ever such a vast and noisy crowd heaved outside Buckingham Palace gates. Yet, there was a dramatic silence when King George V began to speak.

Most vividly, when I recall that day, I see one little lad sitting astride his dad's shoulders, his tiny cap awry, his face grubby and his nose running. Cocking his head and holding up his forefinger, he said: " 'ark, 'ee, daddy, a band; 'ark, 'ee, daddy, another band".

The queues outside the restaurants seemed to stretch in never ending lines along the paths. When at last we sat down at a table, a waitress announced: "Five shilling tip before I serve anyone". Rules were thrown to the wind. The rows and rows of drunken women, arm in arm across the roads at Vauxhall, their long hair down, reeling and shouting, were not a pretty sight. As we left the bus that brought us back to College, one of the girls – not looking where she was going – fell over a ladder, nearly bringing down the man who was scraping the black from the lamp window. A light began to show in the street that had been dark for so long.

College, on our return, seemed a peaceful spot. A broken chair greeted me in my bedroom. In the excitement of dressing for Town, I had put my foot on its cane bottom to tie my shoelaces with such gusto that the heel went right through. That night, my little balcony was crowded. It was a good vantage post from which to see the fireworks breaking the long years of London's gloom.

30. PROBLEMS WITH RELIGIOUS EDUCATION

At Southlands Training College, although it was run under the auspices of the Methodist Church, I do not remember one word of advice or anything whatever that would help one to teach Scripture to children. What help could have been given? An imaginative syllabus worked out for the young teacher to follow when the time came for her to face a class of her own. What an opportunity lost!

Twice a week we had Divinity. The Chaplain came into the lecture room after stopping in the corridor to ask a student to brush his coat. He had his notebooks under his arm. Then we knew – or most of us did – that we had an hour for letter writing. Over and over again, we would hear the sentence: "Are creeds necessary and useful: are creeds necessary and useful?" Respectfully, I listened to the first few lectures, then I joined the already big number of letter writers.

We took it in turns to find references if one of us was called by name to read from the Bible. One morning, when my name was called, the student 'on duty' passed the Bible along the row. The girl next to me pointed to the verse. I stood and read: "And whether it be a cow or ewe, ye shall not kill it and her young both in one day." What <u>was</u> I reading?

"Thank you," said the Chaplain, quite satisfied. I very much doubt if he had heard me. He continued reading from his notes in the same abstracted manner, never suspecting, it seemed, that our writing was totally unconnected to his 'Divinity'. Occasionally he would say: "It is encouraging to see you taking so many notes!"

When the day approached for the annual Divinity examination, the few – and they were few – who had continued conscientiously to take notes lent them round. I learned them more or less by heart and duly registered them on the examination paper. Result: near

Light, Love, Life: the Southlands Training College motto that Dorothy liked. From Southlands College Archives, University of Surrey Roehampton

maximum marks! This was not exceptional, for others were as good and some had 100%. This exam did not count in any way in the College official exams.

In our senior year, two of us made a pact that we would not learn any notes, but would answer the questions giving our own theological ideas. We did. My friend gained 36%. I beat her with 40%. Some of my answers, I was told, were 'near heresy'. Today they are commonplace. I know that these Divinity questions were the same for five years; for how much longer I can only surmise. If it were possible to have a dozen or so students of my time and to ask them for one thing they remembered from the Divinity lectures, I am sure the unanimous response would be: "Are creeds necessary and useful?"

Many years later, my husband and I used to meet the Minister who had been responsible for marking these papers. I doubt if his humility would have allowed him to question the College Chaplain. Looking at him, I would have loved to tell him that he hadn't thought much of my idea of theology, but I felt it better not to disturb the dust.

Once, when on school practice, I sat with another student marvelling at the story coming from the lips of the teacher. Joseph, David and Daniel were all merged into one man in a story that did at least gain the children's attention. She went on and on, and then, turning to us asked: "What comes next?" We advised her to look it up in her Bible. "That's all for today, children," she said cheerfully: "we'll finish tomorrow." We had been in her classroom for over a week, and had greatly admired her well-prepared lessons on other subjects. Only when it came to Scripture did she show neglect.

At the Grammar School my son attended during World War Two [Barnstaple Grammar School], the boys were given chapters of the Bible to write out as a form of punishment. The master in question would sometimes ridicule Bible stories. He openly admitted he took Religious Instruction against his wish. In my children's time, as in my own, it still seemed to be true that, if time was needed for any extra activity, such as practice for a play, the pupils concerned were kept from morning Prayers.

Such things happened years ago, and we elders cannot pretend that all was well with Scripture teaching in the past. In my day school, we had a chapter of the Bible to prepare for homework, and what a chapter it often was! We never in all the years got around to the New Testament. Twice – and always in the same order – the Headmistress would go round the class, asking questions about Jereboam or Rehoboam, Elijah or Elisha. One might have been able to answer every other question except the two addressed to oneself.

Failure to answer both questions meant a detention. The lesson, lacking any element of inspiration or apparent relevance, left me bored and resentful: the only uninteresting lesson of the week.

And what of the future? The next few years should show some interesting developments.

I gave other subjects their due preparation, but it was lessons on Education and Advanced Education that specially interested me. I responded to anything that dealt with the living child. The books in the Library on child psychology opened up a new world. I devoured them avidly and looked forward to my evening visit to the Library. There I was also introduced to some of the mellow London evening newspapers of that time: the green *Westminster Gazette*, the pink *Globe*. I was surprised that so few students made use of the Library.

One tutor would talk to us by the hour on child psychology. Those of us who took Advanced Education met in her study. Keen as I was on her subject, I still think that, like many propagandists, she carried some ideas too far. She would say that, if a child threw his cup of milk on the floor, you should leave it there until he wanted some more milk and then take him to the broken cup. So far, so good! But she would maintain that, even if the child threw down other cups in his paddy, you should not fuss, remembering the child always comes first.

"China can be replaced, but not a child." I used to sit and wonder what she would be like with several lively youngsters round her tea table. When one of us pointed out that, from the money point of view, one could not carry on like this, sweetly she would smile and answer: "Ah, my dear, you're making the mistake of not putting first things first."

"But I am," said one student: "the first thing is to have a cup to put milk in. You can't afford for a child to break too much." Completely unruffled, the tutor would reply: "Do always remember the child."

This tutor set us a holiday task. It was to make some individual apparatus to help children in their first number lessons. I put many

The College Library. Photo from the publication Retrospect – Prospect, 1872 - 1928, Southlands Training College, Battersea. From Southlands College Archives, University of Surrey Roehampton

hours into my work, thinking it would be useful in my own classes when I left College. Among many other things, I boiled hundreds of plum stones and then painted them in vivid colours. With a gaily-painted tin full of these, the child would have an aid for his first number work. A few days after our holiday work was handed in, I met the tutor in the corridor. She informed me that she was keeping my apparatus to send to an exhibition she was planning. She added: "It is an honour for you." I was aware of no honour, only bitter disappointment.

There was nothing in my effort that could not have been done by anyone willing to give up their time in their holidays. Much time I

119

certainly had given. I asked her if, after the exhibition, I could keep all the individual apparatus for future use, but she declined. It took me many days to get over that loss and a feeling of resentment, for I had not so much as been asked if I would allow the work to go to the exhibition, let alone part with it. Another instance, perhaps, to show that students at this time did not sufficiently stand up for their legitimate rights.

Apart from periods on Education, anyone could have attended normal lectures week after week and have no idea that we were teachers in training. Academic lectures may have soundly furthered the student's own education, but no hint was ever given of how we might foster the imagination of children in any subject. Of course, it was not possible to combine these two aims in the same lectures, but time could have been found for planning syllabuses with the aid of students' own ideas, so that – when a student left College – she had something definite to work on.

Conditions in schools varied. Some headmistresses made their own syllabus for the student teacher to follow, while others left a beginner to fend as best she could for herself. I knew from letters received from former students how sadly some of them floundered when they began to teach in their first school. It still seems strange to me that I would never have approached any tutor in the College, save the Education one, for any advice that would help me as a future teacher. Yes! There was one, our Zoology tutor.

In a few sentences, she could fire your imagination, giving ideas for Nature lessons, which I am sure bore fruit in many classes round the country. Ponds in the garden provided specimens for our aquaria. You could never walk round her laboratory without seeing something of interest. I sat for a very long time watching a dragonfly emerge in all its glory: a memorable afternoon.

There were no young members on the staff, except the Gym tutor. All were resident, apart from the occasional visiting lecturer. One day, Cecil Sharp[1] joined in our country-dances on the lawn. His rhythm was wonderful. He seemed to flow through different movements without effort. Elsie Fogarty came for a series of lectures on voice production[2]. She was a dear character, so individualistic, her hair anything but tidy.

One day she asked me to stay behind when the other students left the hall. She pulled out a hairpin, bent it, and put it in my mouth, asking me to say words after her. She startled me by asking if I would go to her for voice training. I have always loved poetry, but have detested 'elocution' of the type then too often heard at concerts. She asked me again before she finished her course of lectures. But, still only thinking in terms of 'elocution', I once more declined. What have I missed? In a biography of Fogarty, I read that a number of famous actors, and other public men and women, were trained by her.

---

[1] *Longman's Encyclopaedia* 1989 states: "Although it has become fashionable to criticise Sharp's efforts and to forget his genuinely socialist leanings, he was, more than any other single person, responsible for salvaging English Folk Song and Dance and encouraging their performance and further study at a crucial point in the transformation of rural society."

At the time Dorothy met him, he was an Occasional Inspector [for the Board of Education] for teacher training institutions: "And went around inspecting, giving demonstrations, and mostly complaining about what he saw and heard." From the introductory chapter by Vic Gammon in *Still Growing: English Traditional Songs and Singers from the Cecil Sharp Collection* [English Folk Dance & Song Society. 2003].

[2] Elsie Fogarty founded the Central School of Speech and Drama in 1906 to offer an entirely new form of training in speech and drama for young actors and other students [*Prospectus* 2004]. Alumini include Laurence Olivier and Peggy Ashcroft.

32. STUDENT CHAT

On Sunday afternoon, every student was supposed to remain in her own room. One small group at least never kept the rule. We met in one another's rooms, talking and arguing on every subject under the sun: that is on all subjects save one, sex. Repressed? Unhealthy? Immature? That we never were! Naturally, I cannot speak for the whole College, though in the lecture rooms, Common Room or elsewhere, I heard no hint of sex.

I think most, if not all of us, would have expressed the desire to marry (indeed we used light-heartedly to exchange ideas about the 'perfect' husband), but we just had not reached that part of the road. In the meanwhile, we fully enjoyed the present. Most of us were intimate with one or two special friends, but even here sex did not enter into the conversation. It was not that we would have wished to talk about it, but thought it wrong to do so or felt it better to keep quiet about such things. It simply was not on the syllabus of our thoughts. Things would, no doubt, be different today! I merely register a fact. The nearest we ever came to the subject was the question – brought up by meeting mentally defective children from the same family – whether or not sterilization was desirable.

One of our group had received a letter from her father, a master builder, who was having trouble in his firm. For the first time I was brought face to face with the growing strength of trade unions and with the question of restrictive practices. Some of the men in the father's firm had been laying too many bricks. This had caused trouble. It seemed strange to us that anyone should be penalized for doing a bit of extra work. As we talked on, however, we became aware that unemployment was the great fear in the men's minds. As I look back, I can see that this talk, bringing human and psychological factors into focus, was something of a watershed in my outlook. I began to appreciate that problems affecting human relationships are many sided.

At this time, equal pay for men and women teachers was beginning to be discussed. There was one senior student who crusaded for equal pay whenever she had the chance to raise her voice. I do not think the majority of students at that time were much moved one way or the other. I was not in favour of it, thinking that in most cases the man bore the financial burden. But, here again, the complexity of the matter, if not the fairness, has over the years changed one's mind.

The majority of students came from religious homes, or at least from homes where institutional religion was accepted as the norm. From childhood, they had unquestioningly attended church, for morning and evening services on Sunday and also for weeknight meetings. Now, for the first time, some began to exercise their own minds. They certainly had no wish to break with the Church. It was the dogmatic insistence on certain fixed ideas and forms that disturbed them.

A few students were not merely worried, they were positively distressed. They felt that any change in their own church habits was good-bye to God for them. Seeing Him only in fixed terms, and now finding these terms challenged, they could have said like Mary at the empty tomb: "They have taken away my Lord, and I do not know where they have laid Him."

Our arguments were long and frank, yet always friendly. What was the Church? Was it a building in which the religious gathered at specified times for formal worship, or should it be a living, unlimited community of believers? Or to what extent could these two concepts be reconciled? And when one Church hardly recognized another denomination as Christian, where were we? These and many other problems we discussed and, whatever else we might be ready to doubt, there was never any question of abandoning faith altogether.

It was the rule of the College that all students should attend the local Methodist Church except for two Sundays in each term, when they were free – if they wished – to worship elsewhere. In any institution, there should not be too many rules but what there are

College friends in grounds of Southlands Training College. The centre student is Dorothy. The photo is a useful glimpse into life of students at that time when not many photos were taken

should surely be enforced. It remains a mystery why this rule about two free Sundays should have been so flagrantly broken by some of us. It was all done openly, but we were never once challenged.

We attended the local Church for the first Sunday in the term or if, very occasionally, there was a special preacher. For the rest, with one or two friends, I went to Westminster Abbey, the Central Hall, Westminster Chapel, the City Temple, Brompton Oratory and more.

Another rule – a list went up on the notice board – allotted two bath periods a week to each student. Here again, the same few of us slipped upstairs for a bath every evening, and nothing was ever said. There were always plenty of baths and hot water available, so we were not penalizing other students. The Zoology tutor, whose over-mastering passion was for hygiene, would sometimes meet us on the stairs as she came from her study, and with a twinkle in her eye would say: "Keep up the good work."

Dorothy (right) with two College friends on holiday

Dorothy (right) with College friend. Venue unknown

33. COLLEGE ENDS

Toward the end of the two years, there was the big question: where were all the students, not only in our College but also in all the other training colleges, going to teach? A student applied to the County of her choice. Then, at a given time, representatives from all over the country came to interview students in the Colleges. If a student was not accepted for the County of her first choice, she applied elsewhere.

At this time, there were four scales of payment. London, for instance, had Scale I. We in Kent were on Scale II. Unless it was their home ground, students were not keen to apply for a post, say, in Devon to which Scale IV applied. A uniform scale came into operation after the Second World War. Headmasters or Headmistresses have always been paid according to the size of their school, which has a group number. There are, however, considerably more than four of these groups.

One evening, all the students stretched in a long queue from the Principal's study down to the Main Corridor. One by one we entered her room to sign an agreement that we would teach at least five years after we had finished training. If, for marriage or any other reason, the contract was broken, some repayment had to be made. There are no such conditions today.

I accepted the offer to join the staff of the school in my home town, where I had been a pupil teacher[1]. I had very mixed feelings. Part of me felt that I should have the courage to seek new pastures. Some may think that 'courage' is a strange word in this context. I think I could have faced adversity with the best, but I clung to the known and familiar. The ordinary day-to-day routine has brought more happiness through the years than have times of change and excitement. I knew that after the life of the last two years I should

---

1 The Hythe [Council] Girls' School.

Miss Brunyate, Principal, during Dorothy's time at College. From Southlands College Archives, University of Surrey Roehampton

feel the limitations of a small town. Then, there would be times when it was difficult to be natural.

If you enjoyed an occasional intelligent conversation with a man, tongues would begin to wag. Friendships that might have ripened into something deeper were frustrated by silly gossip. I envy students of today one thing. How I should have loved to try different jobs in the holidays: something unheard of in my time.

The two years at College had been happy years, not least through friendships made. I thought then, as I still think, that much could have been done to send us out into the teaching world armed with more effectual aids for our work. Yet, I was grateful for what College had offered me. Horizons had broadened: life was happy and rewarding. It seemed a pity that the warmth and companionship collapsed so suddenly at the end.

It would have been good if all students could have stayed on a few extra days and then all have departed together. As it was, everyone left as soon as she had finished her own subjects. College by the time I left was nearly empty. Rooms and corridors so recently agog with activity were now almost eerily silent.

The College Hall. Photo from the publication Retrospect – Prospect 1872 - 1928, Southlands Training College, Battersea. From Southlands College Archives, University of Surrey Roehampton

The architecturally beautiful hall was deserted. Every day we had sat facing the stained glass window bearing Coleridge's lines:

O'er wayward childhood wouldst thou hold firm rule,
And sun thee in the light of happy faces?
Love, Hope, and Patience, these must be thy graces,
And in thine own heart let them first keep school.

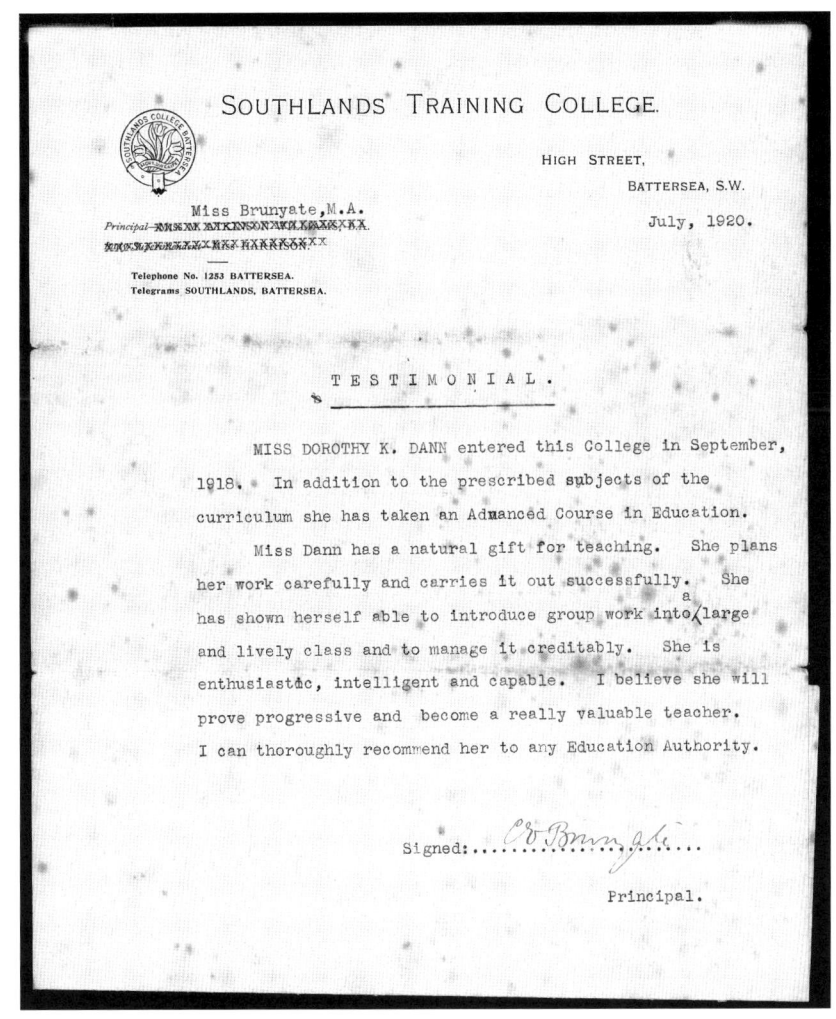

SOUTHLANDS TRAINING COLLEGE.

HIGH STREET,
BATTERSEA, S.W.

Miss Brunyate,M.A.
Principal

July, 1920.

Telephone No. 1283 BATTERSEA.
Telegrams SOUTHLANDS, BATTERSEA.

T E S T I M O N I A L .

MISS DOROTHY K. DANN entered this College in September, 1918. In addition to the prescribed subjects of the curriculum she has taken an Advanced Course in Education.

Miss Dann has a natural gift for teaching. She plans her work carefully and carries it out successfully. She has shown herself able to introduce group work into a large and lively class and to manage it creditably. She is enthusiastic, intelligent and capable. I believe she will prove progressive and become a really valuable teacher. I can thoroughly recommend her to any Education Authority.

Signed:.....................

Principal.

Testimonial of Dorothy's completing two years at Southlands Training College

129

Whenever I travelled home through the Kentish countryside, I enjoyed afresh its peace. With luck, you could almost be sure of a compartment to yourself. Whether the orchards were in bloom, the cherries or apples being harvested, the hop poles bare in spring or garlanded in late summer, I felt pride in 'this blessed spot'.

On the day I left College, my bits and bobs were indeed a strange collection. A young woman can gather much together in two years! Due to its being the holiday season, there were more passengers on the train from Charing Cross. Having deposited my junk on the rack, I sat in a corner seat, ready for the journey home and the beginning of a new chapter.

We made the normal longish stop at Tonbridge: then away. Soon we were slowing down. Being familiar with every station on that South Eastern and Chatham Railway from London to Folkestone, I exclaimed to my startled fellow passengers: "We are at Tunbridge Wells." "Can't be," said an elderly man sitting in the opposite corner and, looking over the top of his newspaper, then said: "This is the Folkestone line, not the Hastings." "I know Tunbridge Wells station," I said in no uncertain voice.

I was already gathering my belongings and was soon off the train, up the steps and over the bridge. The collector at the end asked for my ticket. I tried to explain but he refused to listen. "Met the likes of you before," he said. I told him I would wait. He would soon see the other passengers. Immediately, they swept round the end of the bridge and came toward us. He looked dumbfounded. Turning to me, he apologized profusely.

We all went down the steps on to the other platform to await a train to take us back to Tonbridge. The only time the railways have given me a free ride! Whoever had been responsible for the uncoupling at

Tonbridge had left our coach attached to the Hastings portion of the train. I chuckled to myself as I sat on the platform, hoping this was no ill omen for myself. About to start on my career, I had no wish to take the wrong track.

I expected to begin work after the summer holidays, but soon after reaching home I was asked if I would supply-teach for the next two weeks, the last of the term. I had not thought of payment, and was surprised to be told that I had been placed on the permanent staff. This meant teaching for a fortnight and then receiving salary for the five weeks' holiday. I doubt if this would be done today. Naturally I was pleased when the monthly cheque arrived, but I thought the authorities were over-indulgent, if not a bit stupid.

A few days before I received the cheque, Mother and I, while shopping, had much admired a tea service on show in a china shop. I bought this with my first full purse: that was fifty two years ago. We have just used it for tea today. It was some time before my cheque grew bigger. Salaries were cut by 5% soon after the War (strange reading today!). Then a superannuation scheme was introduced, which meant another 5% salary cut.

When you have lived all your life in a small town it is surprising how you recognize a family resemblance in a child. Over and over again, I would say to a boy or girl: "Is your mother's name so-and-so?" The answer would often be 'Yes' or 'No, that's my aunt'. Children and even grandchildren of boys and girls I had taught were often recognized when I went home for holidays in later years. How stubborn is heredity!

Knowing the staff and the School, I began my first term as a fully fledged teacher with little apprehension. The senior member of the staff had now become Head, teaching full-time a class of her own. There were five of us, a friendly, happy group.

The one thing I had wanted above all else from the final College examination was a Credit in the Advanced Course in the Principles

BOARD OF EDUCATION.

THIS IS TO CERTIFY

that *Dorothy Kathleen Dann* was trained at the *London, Battersea, Southlands Training College* for two years from 19*/8*to 19*20*; that she passed the Board's Final Examination for Students in Training Colleges in 19*20*, and in other respects completed her Course of Training satisfactorily; and that she is recognised by the Board under the Code of Regulations for Public Elementary Schools as a Certificated Teacher, from *1st August 1920.*

Subjects included in the Student's Course of Study.	*The Principles and Practice of Teaching; Hygiene; Theory of Music and Singing; Physical Training; Reading and Recitation; Drawing; Needlework; English; Geography; Elementary Science.—*
Subjects in which the Student passed with credit.	*The Principles and Practice of Teaching (Advanced Course).—*

H. A. L. Fisher

President.

Edmund Phipps

Principal Assistant Secretary,
Elementary Education Branch.

This Certificate will be endorsed when the Teacher has completed a year's service in Elementary Schools as required by the Code for that purpose.

Endorsed accordingly.

18th January 1922. Edmund Phipps

Dorothy's Board of Education teaching certificate. This was endorsed and issued after teaching at least one year in 'Elementary Schools as required by the Code for that purpose'

and Practice of Teaching. With one other student in my year, I pulled this off. I am sure that all the practical work I had done as a Pupil Teacher had stood me in good stead.

Letters from some College friends told of disappointments in their first schools. Their Heads, adamant in their ways of teaching, allowed no freedom or initiative. It was one thing to leave Training College with enthusiasm for your work; it was quite another thing to have every new suggestion squashed and to be compelled to fall in with the curriculum as it had been for many a long day. My own Head was not of the type who thought herself always right. She would accept a new idea, once she saw good reason for doing so.

It is strange how, in all walks of life, certain ideas and conditions stubbornly persist when one would have thought mere commonsense would long ago have shaken belief in them. Generation after generation of teachers had stood before their classes the whole day through. Never, never would they have dreamed of sitting down! Were old-fashioned notions of authority involved? Was it assumed that the standing teacher inspired more respect? Was it thought that he or she was better able to maintain discipline? Or did sitting smack too much of slovenliness and laziness?

I don't think I ever sat while taking a lesson before going to College. Then, after it was pointed out, I could see the folly of standing in front of small children to tell a story. Your face was far above their eye level; sitting down you became one of them, creating a much more friendly atmosphere. So I now sat when it seemed appropriate, albeit somewhat uneasily. I was conscious that the Head was not quite at home with this innovation. We talked it over. She, too, was soon following suit.

I remember only one other disagreement. I had a left-handed girl in my class; there was no doubt about this. Whenever the Head came into the room and saw the child using her left hand she would insist on her changing to the right. I tried to explain – with my newly acquired knowledge! – that it would probably cause stuttering and a general upset for the girl. The Head was sure this could not be so. I could not let the girl use her left hand and, in front of her, I had been told that the right hand must always be used. It was not long before the fair-haired seven-year old began to stutter badly. She was then allowed to use her left hand and returned to normal.

At this time, 1920, some children were received into school before their fifth birthday, if numbers permitted. These very young children had their hammocks, which were quickly put up every afternoon for them to lie on. Quite a number of them would sleep.

The first day of the term, especially the autumn term, which brought a bigger number of new children, saw interesting play between mothers and children. Most children cheerfully left mum to take their first step in school life. Some were a little, quietly weepy. A few clung, yelling, to mum. This was generally caused by the mother's possessiveness. She did not like, or even think it right, that the child should part too easily from her. We were always glad when this type of mum departed, for the child was soon happy, playing with other children.

35. CLASSES WERE BIG

Classes were big: forty-plus pupils, boys and girls. Even with so large a class, much as one might have wished it smaller, it was possible to give some individual attention. It meant hard, very hard, work, but it could be done. We had to see that the children were up to a certain standard by the time they reached the age for the senior schools, that was seven to eight years.

This getting the children to a certain stage with their work by a given time had its advantages as well as disadvantages. Of course, some youngsters easily reached a higher standard than others. The danger was that some teachers might push a slow child beyond his capacity. But all, at least, had a fair chance and a fair share of the teachers' time. We did not consider it right that a bright child should receive more attention than a slow one. The system certainly allowed no slacking on the teacher's part.

I wish it were possible to take some present-day teachers back to this school. They would not find all the teaching and methods antiquated, as they may assume them to have been. As I have said before, the classrooms were then quieter, but our visitors would find that quite a bit of our practice corresponded with their own. We had our occasional open days, when parents wandered at will, watching the boys and girls at work and talking to them.

They saw them at games, physical exercises and dancing. The walls, covered with paintings and drawings – the Handwork also – provided evidence of the children's initiative. On Friday afternoons, youngsters brought their own toys. When weather permitted, they played outside. If it was too cold or wet, classrooms and hall were thrown open for free moving around. The very young enjoyed a large sandpit.

Family and friends picnic on Hythe beach 1921. I believe Dorothy took this photo. Standing left to right: Robert Dann with granddaughter Pauline also being held by her mother Maud, May, ?, ?, Violet holding Daisy's child Barbara, ?. Sitting left to

Classes were divided into groups according to ability. Thus, in reading, Group 1 was free to use books from a small library. The children in Group 2 would each be reading a copy of the same book and, at the end of the period, would ask the teacher if help was needed. Group 3 worked with the teacher who, as soon as she thought a child capable of reading on his own, would let him join Group 2.

I often found that an apparently normal, bright child made little progress with reading because he was held back by lack of confidence. A short time with me on his own, before or after school and never with a hint of punishment, soon made a big difference. Once confidence was gained there was no further trouble.

After half-a-century, I still remember some of the children. There were, as in every school, those who tried hard, plodded along but showed little originality. Take Bill, a loveable, cheery lad; it seemed as if he would go through life with a very limited vocabulary. I just could not get him to introduce a new word into his conversation or writing. By the look on his face, when I tried to do so, I might have suggested something positively wicked. He lived in a happy home and nothing gave him more pleasure than to speak or write of it. The story of his family would read like this: "I like my mum, I like my dad. My dad likes me. My mum likes me. My dad likes my mum. My mum likes my dad. We like the dog. We all likes all."

Domestic bliss indeed! I wondered if Bill ever developed enough to write a more exciting letter to his lady love. Other children, having heard a new word, immediately adopted it. Jill did so when, for the first time, she learned the meaning of 'handsome'. Up shot her hand to prove that she understood. "My mum," she volunteered: " 'as a 'andsome 'at."

The apparent injustices of life show at an early age. Some boys and girls do excellent work with little effort, while others, for all their trying, reach only a poor standard. If today I could see those children grown-up, should I be surprised to find which of them, by conventional standards of ability, had made the grade? It was nothing unusual for us to see a slow beginner, and don't let us equate him with the lazy child, forging ahead in the senior school.

It has always been the same. Four hundred years ago, Roger Ascham, in *The Scholemaster*, suggested that teachers, when confronted with an apparently bright child and an apparently dull one, should: "discreetly consider the right disposition of both their natures, and not so much way [weigh] what either of them is able to do now as what either of them is likely to do hereafter. For this I know, not only by reading of books in my study, but also by experience of life abroad in the world, that those which be commonly the wisest, the best learned, and the best men also, when they be old, were never commonly the quickest of wits when they were young".

A studio photo of Dorothy when she was in her early 20s and teaching in Hythe

Dorothy (centre) on holiday in Barmouth with her College friend Gwen, who took this photo. Charlie Boothroyd (left) married Gwen and Donald (right) was a friend of Dorothy's. This foursome travelled by motorcycles. Gwen later lived in Sheffield and she and Dorothy visited each other with their children for many years

36. "AIN'T GOD LAZY, MISS?"

When I spent a holiday in Sheffield with Gwen, a College friend, I first realized the difference in the relationship between teachers that taught in large and small towns. My friend would leave her class on Friday afternoon and not see one of the children again until Monday morning. That, I now realized, was normal for very many teachers. On the other hand, in a small town, whether you walked by the sea or in the country, went to church or a concert or anywhere else, some bright-eyed youngsters would be grinning at you. Not only did you become more friendly with the children, you got to know their parents. Thus the interests of the school and home were brought together.

Parents sometimes made unusual requests. There was a mother who could not get her girl to take her malt and cod liver oil, then the recognized panacea for many juvenile ailments. Would I mind keeping the jar in my classroom cupboard and seeing that Phyllis had her dose twice daily? Phyllis took it like a lamb and seemed thoroughly to enjoy it. How often children who are little angels at school are little something-elses at home and vice versa!

Occasionally a mother would ask if, in the course of normal conversation, I could try to find out what was worrying her boy or girl. Why is it children who jabber about everyday things so freely stop short of asking a question that could be simply answered and so set their minds at rest. Are they afraid of the answers? Even at their age, may pride enter into it? May the very near relationship cause a shyness of its own?

Once when young, I suffered unnecessary hours of misery after hearing a hymn in church. "Cleanse me by water or by fire," the congregation had sung. What was this cleansing by fire? I lay in bed wondering how it would come to me. If there was a thunderstorm, I was terrified lest the lightning should come to cleanse my body. Then, when visiting Dover, I saw an advertisement in one of the

Party to celebrate Martha Dann's sixty-fifth birthday in 1922. The photo was taken on the bank of the Military Canal, Hythe. Back row left to right: Robert Dann, Dorothy, ? , Brian with his mother Daisy, her husband Ralph, and May. Middle row: friend of Emmeline's, Martha and two of her friends. Front row left to right: Emmeline, Barbara and Lily

small electric trams of a man in a Turkish bath. I knew immediately – or thought I did – that he was being cleansed by fire. The flames, not coming too near his body, were taking all his dirt away. Why, even in homes as happy as mine was, did children jib at revealing their thoughts?

Seven-year-old Ted, at any rate, had no inhibitions. He came up to me one morning and said bluntly with great assurance: "Ain't God lazy, Miss?" I began to speak to him but, interrupting, he confidently assured me that God was lazy. I tried to get in a few more words, but again was stopped. "Crickey, Miss, fancy only being able to unlock a gate; coo! I can do more than that." At morning prayers in school, we had sung *There is a green hill far away*. Ted had got his emphasis wrong in the words: "He only can unlock the gates of Heaven."

140

For the children, there were occasionally embarrassing moments when they could have wished their teachers miles away. One Saturday, I chanced to see a skylark's nest and called three of my young hopefuls, who happened to be near, to come and look at the brown speckled eggs. They promised me that none would be taken. A little later, I passed that spot again, and found the nest empty. I met the lads on my way home. "No, Miss, we have not touched the eggs."

"What's that under there, George, I said? And put my hand on his suspicious looking cap [a favourite place for 'hiding' eggs]. Immediately, little yellow streams ran down his face. Poor George! Who would have believed that four wee skylark's eggs could have made such a mess. We cleaned him up in a nearby stream. George faced me on Monday morning with a nervous grin.

"Well, George," I said: "four skylarks won't be singing in the sky this summer, will they?" "Why not, Miss?"

"Broken eggs can't sing, can they George?" He now saw the point and had a good laugh. I had the feeling he had taken his last egg out of a nest.

37. SCHOOL TRIP TO LONDON

Early one summer morning, nearly a thousand children from the Senior Schools in our area travelled by special train to London for the day. Apart from sharing the same train, each school made its own arrangements. I had gone to help the Senior Headmaster and his staff with our local children. Each teacher was responsible for his or her own group: I had twelve girls of eleven years. The Head asked me to keep my group at the end of the queue and on no account to move forward till everyone in front was walking on. This sounded simple enough, but it turned out to be little less than a race round London.

I knew vaguely that if successive groups of people in a long queue were each in turn to stop at a given place for a short time, and then to move on, those toward the end would have an ever-increasing rush to catch up. How true this now proved!

My girls had seen so little; the morning had been disappointing. We ended up at the Zoo for an early lunch, which the children had brought with them. We all sat on the grass, thankful for a rest. Determined that this visit to London – the first for nine of the girls – should be a day for them to remember happily, I went to find the Head. I told him that I would be responsible for my party in the afternoon and would be on time for the booked tea at the ABC café in Whitehall. To my surprise he agreed immediately.

The afternoon more than compensated for the morning. No sightseers to the Capital ever squeezed more into a few hours. Our last 'call' was Buckingham Palace. As we stood at the gates, King George and Queen Mary came out in their car. "You did plan that well, Miss," said one lass. After tea the School party made its way to Charing Cross. Helen had been anxious to take home a small present for mum, but there had been no time for shopping.

As we walked into the station, she bought one red rosebud from the flower woman standing in the entrance. The girl asked if it could be wrapped in tissue paper. The rosebud cost nine pence; a lot of money for a girl in 1925.

When we were all seated in our railway compartment, I said: "Would you like to take your shoes off?" No suggestion was ever carried out more promptly!

The precious rose had been laid carefully on the rack. At intervals on the journey home, it was taken down, unwrapped, smelled, wrapped up again and tenderly returned to the rack. Mum was waiting on the platform for us. She was delighted with her gift: "All the way from London. It cost nine pence, Mum."

"It would, dear, in London."

So the tired but happy travellers dispersed. I began my long walk home. Did I hear a welcome sound? Turning round, I saw the station bus, with its two prancing horses, coming down the hill. The seat outside by the rosy-faced driver was empty. Thankfully, I obeyed his: "Up you get, Miss."

Twenty-five years later, when I was on holiday in my home town, a woman with her husband and children, recognizing me, crossed the road to speak. Laughingly she said: "Do your remember my nine-penny red rose?" Special days were rare for children earlier in the century; all the more were they enjoyed in anticipation and, when over, never forgotten.

The classrooms, heated by huge fires with tall guards, had a homely atmosphere. The caretaker lit the fires early in the morning and made them up again in the dinner hour. But if we needed any more coal, we could always fill the scuttle from the cellar at the end of the hall. No part of the rooms was ever chilly. Some children had long walks and in bad weather arrived very wet. There were boys and girls who had to come a very long distance on the exposed Dymchurch marsh road. Seldom were they late and always arrived cheerfully. They never seemed more tired than the other children. Their wet clothes dried on the fireguard and extra dry socks were kept at school. What a help a school bus and school dinners would have been to them.

When Christmas was near, the whole class joined in helping to make an enormous pudding, talking all the while of the countries and their peoples from which the many ingredients came. Safely in its great basin and tied up, the pudding went into a massive saucepan. It sat on an iron trivet by the side of the fire. Here it boiled and bubbled and bubbled the hours away. The naughtiest boy in the class came up to me the day after it was cooked, saying: "I do miss the bubbling, wasn't it nice?" I was surprised that the tough little rascal should ever have noticed it. There was great excitement when at last the pudding was turned out, cut and tasted.

School inspectors gave no warning of their approach, though messages went round, as if by magic, when one had been spotted. At this time various experiments were being made in methods of teaching the young. With the best will in the world, it was not always easy to keep up with the changes. Any method demands a certain time before it can be determined whether it is sound or not.

An inspector at this time had a very yellow skin. She was known as the Yellow Peril. One of her ideas was that no lesson for the very young should last for more than five minutes. That method didn't last long! If she criticized something you were doing, and you reminded her that she had suggested it on her last visit, she would say: "Oh, things have changed, that was a few months ago!"

The upper halves of our classroom doors were of glass. I would look through mine to see the clock in the hall. Then one morning, between the clock and myself stood the Yellow Peril. My room was near the front door. She had entered and no spy had seen her. Immediately she walked to the far side of the class, away from the door, and began to look at the children's work. On a paper I wrote: "Yellow Peril here," and gave it to a girl sitting near the door to take to the Head. With a knowing expression on her face, the girl returned and whispered to me: "I have been to all the rooms." She knew well why the Head had sent her all round the School. Youngsters are not slow in sizing up a situation.

"There shall never be one lost good." I had always believed this, but a day came when I was tempted to wonder. The Infants', but not the Senior Schools, had an afternoon's holiday. The Head of the Boys' School asked if I would be responsible for his wife's class, to free her for a family party. This class was the one our boys entered on leaving us. It would be interesting, I thought, to see how they were getting on. I was shocked. Their books were covered with blots and smudges. Instead of progressing during the year, their work had deteriorated. A feeling of 'Don't Care' pervaded the room. Every infant teacher in turn had helped those lads. Had all our efforts been in vain, or hadn't they?

One thing that was very different in the schools, especially in the infants', during the years of which I am writing was the closing of the premises during epidemics, when attendance fell low. As this was before the time of inoculation, except for smallpox, illness such as measles, chicken pox, whooping cough and mumps spread very quickly, and often one followed upon the other.

I remember on one occasion when I had forty children in class on a Friday afternoon, and on Monday morning there were only fourteen. This time it was measles. There would be no school for one or two weeks.

Then, when we reassembled, if numbers were still very low, the school would be closed for another week or so. In one year for sickness, we had six consecutive weeks away from school. This rule lasted for many years. It ended about 1923.

Dorothy helping to prepare for a local event, Hythe c1924

39. TIME FOR A CHANGE

After five years, I felt the time had come to make a change and to get more experience. Some friends had moved to Romford, Essex, and I decided to apply for a school in that area. Romford, only thirteen miles from London, was still a quiet market town. It was just beginning to wake from its long past.

There were two old coaching inns but no café. Anyone wanting a cup of tea could sit at a small marble table at the confectioner's. Some of the shops had a Cranfordian air; at one in particular I felt I was being served by Miss Matty herself.

The broad Market Place, with the Church tower on one side, woke into life on Wednesdays, when the cattle and general market brought in folk from miles around. Some of these rustics had never been to London. For them, it remained the great beyond.

Prices at the stalls were very low. At the end of the day a large bunch of bananas, as many as forty of them – those small, full-flavoured Canary ones that we do not see today – were yours for sixpence. Lovely plums cost a penny a pound, thirteen pounds for a shilling, given to you in a market-gardener's strong round basket with a cheery: "Bring it back next week, Madam."

Except in the London direction, the countryside was as tranquil as any to be found in England. Very soon the whole district was to change. Suddenly, at a phenomenal pace, Suburbia thrust itself out. The coming of Ford's to Dagenham[1] hastened the process.

---

[1] Henry Ford's company bought a 500-acre site from S Williams at Dagenham in 1925, the year Dorothy started teaching at Becontree. This development was independent of the London County Council. The LCC sought to keep its Becontree Estate separate, with Ford workers transferring from Manchester in 1931 initially not eligible for its housing. But that was to change, and Becontree residents found work in the new plant, which opened in 1929. Dorothy – by then – was married. [Facts from *A Township Complete in Itself: A Planning History of the Becontree/Dagenham Estate* by Dr Robert Home [University of East London. 1997.]

Romford Market c1910. There was little significant change in the Market Pace for many years except, in the 1920s, a gradual increase in traffic. The Coach and Bell is on the left of the photo. Photo: The London Borough of Havering Library Service

Peaceful walks were snatched away, it seemed, almost overnight. Multiple shops appeared in the main street.

One old Romfordian wasn't going to be caught napping. He ran a small stationer's shop. Without warning a multiple stationery firm opened a branch next door. Some days later, standing on the opposite side of the street – tree-lined, like others at that time – I stared and stared. The small stationer's shop was such no longer. Outside were hung baths, buckets, saucepans and all the other paraphernalia of an ironmonger. The owner, with his hands on hips, stood at his door smiling and confident. This was his native town. No invader was going to push him out of business.

My new school was at Becontree. The bus route from Romford passed fields where boys still walked up and down, frightening the birds off the crops with clappers. Whatever the weather, I sat on the open top deck. A heavy leather apron hung behind every seat. In

148

wet weather, this apron could be unhooked and put over one's lap. It was eerie when we crawled through thick fog. I must have been crazy; still, I never had a cold.

At Becontree, homes were being provided for many who had lived in the East End slums now being cleared by the London County Council. The school was built to serve this vast housing estate, one of the first of its kind. It was a very pleasant estate, with red brick houses and wide roads. Here and there were groups of shrubs. Small front gardens, cherished by the tenants who had not previously possessed a plot of their own, flourished.

The first time I walked to my new school, with two other teachers from the bus that we left on the Chadwell Heath main road, I marvelled at the number of children running out of the houses[2]. The whole area teemed with young life. On the opening day of the new Methodist Central Hall, over eight hundred boys and girls turned up for Sunday school. A few teachers could do little. At the evening service, there were only a handful of adults. The church was far too big. Times were changing.

Congregations were already diminishing. But here, in a large estate, where there were children in every house, and where (apart from any other reason) dad and mum wished for a quiet Sunday afternoon, the youngsters flocked to Sunday school. The family car was not yet with us. I was interested recently to hear on the radio that, at Becontree, as on a similar estate at Dagenham, the community was now mainly an ageing one, bringing different problems.

---

2   I have not been able to trace the name of the School where Dorothy taught. It was obviously on the north [Chadwell Heath] side where building of the Becontree Estate began. Between 1921 – 1924, 3,296 houses were completed, and the rate of house-building accelerated from then. Becontree was to become the largest Council estate in Europe. The name Becontree is not much used now: ". . . but it survives in the historical record as a massive social experiment which rehoused over a hundred thousand people from inner London to the Essex countryside" [Dr Robert Home].

Hythe Girls' School
Kent.
Sep. 22nd 1925.

I have very much pleasure in writing this testimonial for Miss Dorothy Dann, whom I have known all her life.

Miss Dann served her apprenticeship under my supervision and from the very beginning of her teaching career, proved herself a teacher of more than average ability. Her work has always been carried out in a thorough and conscientious manner and her methods marked by brightness and originality. Many girls have been admitted to this School who have been taught by Miss Dann and there has been abundant evidence of the careful training they have received, not only in the ordinary rudiments of education but also in the formation of good morals. Miss Dann has a charming personality and has won the love of her scholars and the esteem and respect of her colleagues. I can confidently recommend her for the post she is seeking.

Strouse. L. L. A.
(Head Mistress).

The two references Dorothy received for her teaching in Hythe. They were passed to her new school on the Becontree Estate. Hythe Council School and Hythe Girls' School were the same school

150

Council School,
Hythe. Kent.
Sep: 22nd 1925

Miss D. K. Dann has been on
the Staff of the above School since
leaving College in July 1920; and
during this time, has given every
satisfaction. She has had charge of
Standard I and Classes I & II.
She is extremely conscientious in her
work, and very painstaking. She
takes a great interest in her scholars,
and is a good disciplinarian, with a
quiet kindly manner to which the
children readily respond. Her class
work has been good at all times,
and the happiest results have been
achieved, particularly with the
retarded children. I shall be
sorry to lose her services.

Signed
Annie E. M. Bates

151

40. MY NEW SCHOOL AT BECONTREE

The School – a pioneer one of its type – was built round an open rectangle with its grass and flowers. Our Infants' classrooms – we had a staff of eight – faced the road. The Senior Boys' and Girls' were on the other side of the rectangle. As I walked into my new classroom, where one whole side was glass, I wondered what distraction the children would find, looking out on a busy thoroughfare.

I need not have worried. It was the teacher who was distracted when – as they were fairly frequent on a route to the cemetery and new to me – the spectacular funerals passed by, often with four heavily plumed black horses drawing the hearse and with paid mourners walking beside it.

The corridors were at times extremely windy. Whenever the classroom door was open any loose papers on the desks were blown on to the floor. It became necessary to enclose the corridors with more glass panelling. One day, when the wind made our door extra hard to push open, I exclaimed: "Oh, this wind!" A five-year old, walking down the corridor, smiled up at me and said: "Mummy says that's what our baby's got, Miss."

At Training College, I had enjoyed a little of the Cockney kids' company. It was good to be with them again. I found them bright and cheerful, quick to help one in trouble; a great spirit of comradeship and fair play prevailed. There was not the same intimacy between the parents and school as I had known before in a small town. Few mums came to meet their offspring. Since most of the houses were quite near, there was little reason to do so from the safety point of view. I did visit some houses when children were sick. There were great contrasts between one home and another when the estate was new.

Next door to a house where everything was tasteful and lovingly arranged, there might be one where, until money could be found for furniture, there was little more than a few upturned boxes. One dad had cut holes in the floorboards. His children's small legs went down the holes, so that the floor served as a table.

What pride some of the women took in their new homes!

As they had been in Hythe, my children in Becontree were seven-plus: the top class in the Infants'. It was interesting to compare the work and characteristics of youngsters in the two schools, brought up in such different environments. I found the Becontree children quicker at their number lessons, most of them grasped a new rule without difficulty. There wasn't a lazy child among them. Their stories and simple essays were more alive. I learned that a Cockney's child's imagination knows no bounds. Nature talks demanded care on my part. I could no longer take it for granted, as I previously had done, that the children knew our native flowers, birds and animals. Now that they had come to live near the country, however, this knowledge began to grow.

Years later we found, when many children were evacuated to us in South Devon, that they were ignorant in the same way. But they, too, soon became wise about Nature's wonders. I passed a mother and child in a country lane. The child picked a flower from the hedge and asked mum what it was. She did not know. I stopped to speak to them and said it was honeysuckle. "Oh, just fancy," said mum: "it's honeysuckle, I never thought we would pick any of that."

At Becontree, I had constantly to remind myself that – until recently – the children had been strangers to open spaces, except the occasional excursion to Epping Forest. One lad, who had moved from an inner London slum a few days before, told me he had never seen a sheep in a field. "Seen one hanging in the butcher's, Miss!" Whereas other children I had taught enjoyed stories of primitive man and our well-known history tales, these children, especially the boys positively lapped them up. It was no uncommon thing to hear:

"Let's have it again, Miss." I suppose I taught these children at a vital stage in their lives. Their environment had suddenly changed, and how they were enjoying it!

I found with many boys and girls in this class that it was a good plan to begin with some Handwork with them and leave them to finish or add to their work in their own way. Their imaginations and fingers produced wonders. Oblivious to what was going on around them, they lost themselves completely in their task. Original pictures were made, or sometimes one was copied from a reading book, by sticking things of very different types on to paper. Today, they would be making a 'collage'. These boys and girls called it: "having a good old stick-up". I have often thought what marvellous artistic work would be achieved in adult life if the promise shown by children went on progressing as they grew up.

Why in fact doesn't it? I suppose that, in essence, all the answers are to be found in Wordsworth's *Intimations* Ode.

41. TEACHERS DIDN'T STRIKE

Never did one walk less than during the 1926 General Strike, so generous were the car drivers in offering lifts. I could not, however, rely upon getting one in the direction of School at the right time. Cycles were in great demand. I managed to borrow a most ancient one. With a Penny-Farthing and several incredible old crocks, a group of us enjoyed the daily push. I marvelled every morning how we reached the school gate.

Trade union rules forbade passengers to travel in lorries or other working vehicles. Early in the morning a builder's empty lorry pulled up at the side entrance of the School. One of our teachers, who usually travelled by train, crawled out from under the tarpaulin. The driver – her father – quickly drove off and returned to take her home in the same way after school.

For a time, it looked as if the whole teaching profession would join the Strike. Rightly or wrongly, I did not feel I could strike and would, if necessary, come out of the National Union of Teachers. The Head was furious. She wanted the whole school closed. She knew that some of us could keep it going. "Don't you know you'll be teaching with the scum?" she said. The scum? Who were they? Where would they come from? Or were they a figment of her imagination? As the teachers did not strike, we never knew.

The children were all bouncing with life – with one exception. This was Peggy, a tall, nervy child who shook with fear. At times she was incontinent. Speaking to her and trying to find out what it was that frightened her, I became aware that her mother's attitude was the cause. If the girl returned home with wet clothes, mum stormed at her to such an extent she went to pieces. On one afternoon, when we were all settling down to Handwork, a woman's loud voice was heard at the end of the corridor. She repeatedly shouted my name and called out: "Where is she? I'll have her blood. Where is she."

The Head, looking thoroughly scared, hurried into my class. "Go quickly into my room and shut the door. I'll stay here." The voice still calling for my blood came nearer. One look at Peggy told me that she knew that voice. I went into the corridor and came face to face with a tall, good-looking woman.

"You called me." I said: "what can I do for you?" As with the Queen of Sheba, there was no more spirit left in her. She stood dumb. I suggested we should go to the end of the corridor to talk, away from the classroom. When not shouting, she had one of the nicest speaking voices I have ever heard.

"I know I do frighten her dreadfully," the woman admitted: "when I get going." She could not believe that her own behaviour was probably to blame for Peggy's weakness. Nevertheless, she promised to try to be more patient. When I turned back, I had to laugh. I felt I was on a station, seeing a train off, for a teacher's head was looking out from every door along the corridor. The mother was as good as her word. She marvelled that her temper had caused this weakness. The very fearful girl turned into a jolly girl. 'Mum' came regularly to see me. It was a joke between us that she had not come for my blood.

42. A DIFFICULT HEAD TEACHER

The Headmistress was an interesting psychological study. I am sure that fundamentally she was good and kind. Unfortunately, she had become a Woman with One Idea! She had worked out an individual apparatus scheme for teaching number and reading. To get all the apparatus finished became her dominant passion: everything in life had to give way to this. We members of the staff, after a hurried lunch, often printed words and figures, sized, painted and varnished boards, measuring approximately twelve inches by nine. She did not like it when we jibbed at putting in long hours on the work after school.

Her obsession obliterated all other interests. She told me she had not time for friends. I thought of her the other day when reading an essay by Dr W R Matthews, who says: "Really good men can easily fall into error . . . They may serve a cause which is relatively good as if it were the supreme Good, and thus turn it into an idol." An idol indeed the Head's scheme had become. It was impossible to hold a normal conversation with her. At a staff meeting we were told: "I never make a mistake." She asked me if I would become Senior Assistant next to her; but, realizing that we could not work in harmony, I declined.

In Kent, I had been used to having my own monthly cheque. In Essex, one cheque was sent off for the whole staff. One day when it was cashed, the Head left the considerable amount of money on the table in her room, with the door open for anyone, child or adult, walking down the corridor to see. I suggested that this was a bit risky. Her answer again was: "I don't make mistakes". Her mania seemed to change what I am sure was fundamentally an honest nature into one capable at times of doing strange things.

This was the first time I had come into close contact with one who through strain could behave in a thoroughly abnormal way without

Dagenham Heathway, Becontree c1929. Photo: London Borough of Barking and Dagenham

being aware of what she was doing. I found it somewhat frightening. John Masefield said of Shakespeare that: "he was always watching the results of an obsession upon an individual and the people connected with him". He saw that the greatest danger in life lay: "not in weakness of will but in strength of will blinded". How sadly for me the Head demonstrated this truth.

Because, with others, I could not agree to stay on for hours after school, I found she had written in my book a criticism of a geography lesson. It was pretty dreadful! Like any other teacher, needless to say, I could make a mistake: but I had never faced a class unprepared. I was the more resentful because she had damned a lesson she could not have heard, since I had never given it! I went to her room in high dudgeon. She seemed unconscious of the wrong she had done. I gave her the option of obliterating the criticism or of my reporting the matter to the Education Office. It was obliterated.

With other members of staff, I realized I could not stay indefinitely at the School. I therefore put in for a transfer. Then, as I became engaged to be married, I did not press the matter. A week or two later, I saw the Secretary from the local Education Office walking down the corridor to the Head's room. After his departure, the Head came to see me, carrying my class register wide open. Now, I haven't a relative or friend who would say a good word for my handwriting; but no teacher ever kept her register in more apple-pie order.

"Just look at this! Look at your altered figures!" She ran her fingers over the page. I stared at the open register. "But," I said: "there isn't a sign of an alteration."

"Look at that," she said sweeping her hand across the page. I said no more. She shut the register and stormed out of the room, leaving me completely mystified. I quickly stopped the astonished children's chatter. But one bright Cockney lad insisted: "She wasn't half cross, wasn't she, Miss."

Presently the door opened and the Head re-appeared. "Why couldn't you tell me you were leaving?"

So this was the trouble! I explained that, though I had indeed asked for a transfer, I had heard nothing about it, and that – as I was now engaged – I had decided to let things rest. For a moment I saw the real woman. Kindly she said: "Why didn't you tell me?"

Never have I known youngsters quicker to sense an atmosphere. Though they were great individualists, mass feeling could quickly be stirred in them. At times this almost frightened me, because, while I had seen it roused only when they thought someone had been wronged, I feared it might not always be harnessed on the side of right. The day after the Head had been so strange to me in front of the class – the children did not know what it was all about, but I was aware they had registered the fact that I had been unfairly treated – an Inspector visited us. She was very unlike the Yellow Peril. She was kindly, courteous and helpful, ready to ask for advice no less than to give it.

Nicholas Road, Becontree c1930. Photo: London Borough of Barking and Dagenham

The Head, who taught for some hours a week, sometimes took my class for singing. We all went into the hall. Then the Inspector said she would like to hear the class sing with the Head. I sat down leaving her in charge. The singing, normally good under her, was dreadful. The children sounded thoroughly weary and bored. I now knew them well enough to know they were acting.

The Inspector then asked me if I could take them for a couple of songs. When the young monkeys had finished, half of me could have hugged them, the other half given them a good spanking! I had never heard more delightful singing, certainly not from these children, whose beaming faces reflected their enthusiasm.

"Well, you have enjoyed singing those songs," said the Inspector.

"Yes, Miss," came an uninhibited chorus. No mere training could have produced either of these performances. They were the natural response of those shrewd Cockney kids with their keen sense of justice.

43. SORRY TO LEAVE SUCH INTERESTING CHILDREN

Apart from the normal holidays, I went home for the weekend once a month. As soon as I appeared at School on Friday morning in a more respectable dress or costume, I would be greeted with: "Going to the sea, Miss?" And I had to give an account of my doings when we met on Monday morning.

I did not want to leave this School. I should never teach more interesting children. We teachers were happy together and enjoyed discussions in the Staff Room, though there was always the nagging feeling that we had taken too long over lunch and should be getting on with 'The Scheme'. None of us had any personal animus toward the Head – or toward her Scheme or apparatus, which were sound enough. What was impossible, and inevitably caused resentment, was the sheer amount of work on them we were expected to do after teaching all day and in the evening giving up some time to preparation for the morrow.

How difficult is the choice of a Head. From the time I spent on school practice while at Training College, I saw how a Head's personality is stamped on the whole life of the School. Your best teachers do not always make your most successful Heads, neither of necessity do those whose exam results are brilliant. Administrative gifts, while essential, are arid by themselves. An indispensable quality is the capacity of getting on with all types of people and of drawing their best work out of them, which implies the ability to listen to ideas as well as to give them.

Only those who have seen the transformation wrought in a school by a change of Head can fully appreciate the power (if used) for good or ill, for spreading happiness or misery, which resides in a Head. One wonders if better methods of making a choice could not be devised. Some Governors and others who make the selection can lack the necessary perception or may be moved by extraneous considerations.

I was offered a school in Romford itself. I knew that in most respects, it would not compare favourably with the Becontree school, but accepted it for the short time before marriage because I knew I could work there in peace. It was a very old building, though light and airy.

No un-certificated teachers were accepted at this time in any new school, which meant that it was difficult for them to move, unless it was to help in some small country school. Here in this old Romford school, two out of a staff of five were un-certificated, though I doubt if any un-informed person would have guessed the fact.

I thought happily of them in 1945 – I think it was that date – receiving a higher salary after years of hard work on such a low one. All un-certificated teachers were then upgraded.

44. METERED WATER AND THE RETIRED CANE

We were up against a difficulty in this school. Our water was metered. Sometimes complaints would come that too much water was being used. Often a child – generally a boy – when told to go back and wash his hands again would smile at you and say: "You told me not to waste water, Miss." To stand in a cloakroom, by a row of washbasins, and watch young boys 'wash' their hands is really an amusing sight! The tougher the lad, the more gingerly he rubs himself. His hands, so anxious he seems not to hurt them, might well be the frailest china.

This is the only School where I saw a cane used. True, it was wielded without ferocity or animosity. Nevertheless, I thought it a degrading affair for all concerned. One extra small boy, a six-year old, was always in trouble, and a bigger boy was regularly involved with him. These two lads stood in front of the whole school with the Head, a tall woman, holding the cane aloft for all to see. The look on the face of the small boy was one of triumph; that of the bigger boy was more subdued. I nearly disgraced myself in front of the whole School by laughing aloud when suddenly the Head pointed the cane at the midget saying: "And to think, Fred, that you are his uncle"!

After twice witnessing this ceremony, I had a talk with the Head and asked if it could stop. She was quite upset to think that she had caused pain: not to the child or to the School but to me. The cane went into retirement.

Fred interested me. I became convinced that, being so undersized and poor at both work and games, his mind turned to ways of drawing attention to himself. Soon after I was married – the next year – a friend of ours, a solicitor, was telling us of some of his Police Court experiences. He spoke of a very small boy who was always in trouble. The description could fit no other than Fred. A day afterwards while shopping, I saw a tall Policeman standing on the path, talking to Fred, and how tiny the lad looked. By the time I reached them, they had parted and I asked the constable if Fred was still in trouble.

"Not at the moment, but whenever I see him I always give him a few words," he said. Before I had finished my shopping, I met the Policeman again. He said: "Would you believe it, immediately he left me he was at it again?"

Fred's favourite trick was to go into a shop, often a tobacconist's, where a number of customers were waiting to be served. He would edge his way to the counter, stand still for a short time then slide his hand up the side of the counter and over the top and take whatever was handy. He had no wish to keep his prize. As soon as he was out of the shop, he would give the packet of cigarettes, or whatever he took, to a passer-by whether or not he knew them. Over and over again, this was the way Fred's guilt was found out.

I am sure he had no desire for personal material gain. He was proving that despite his limitations, he was capable of doing something, and, unfortunately, no one had the wit to see his need. Modern psychology would say he was boosting his ego.

The Head was a simple, innocent, kindly woman, accustomed – unless challenged – to carry on routine as it always had been. On the other hand, far from resenting new ideas, she positively welcomed them. She seldom had any of her own, except for her garden.

She could not understand why a girl of six should be very naughty at home when she was good at school. We were in the playground. She said: "Just look at her beautifully worked smock. How her mother must love her. Why should she be naughty?"

"What has the finely worked smock got to do with her mother's love?" I asked.

"Well, would you do that for someone if you didn't love them?"

I suggested that the mother might do it for other reasons. She could get possessive enjoyment from seeing her child well dressed. It might feed her pride to hear other mothers talk of her beautiful sewing. "Mind you," I said: "I'm not saying there is any lack of affection on the mother's part. But mums can dress children up for other reasons than love."

"Do you know," the Head would say: "my thoughts never get around to anything like that. Funny, isn't it?"

She would never willingly be unkind to any child, but her lack of vision sometimes brought unhappiness. She would pick on a boy or girl who might have some slight abnormality, and refer to it whenever she was near the child. I am sure she meant to be helpful: to let the child know that she understood.

There was a boy whose father, a Canadian, had died from wounds some years after the War. He had left the boy a considerable sum of money. At regular intervals, this lad would turn up at School in a smart suit and an extra snowy-white collar. We then knew that the mother would call later in the morning to take him to a lawyer in London. "Here comes our millionaire," the Head would say when the boy appeared. Again, she was out to show her interest in the lad, but the inevitable result was his being teased by the older children and being made thoroughly unhappy. He was too young to draw any satisfaction from money he would not have until he was grown up. He needed to be one with the other boys. Well may John Masefield say:

Lord give to men who are old and rougher
The things that little children suffer.

166

45. RAZOR BLADES IN THE ROMFORD PLAYGROUND

Discipline was put to a grim test on one occasion. I was on playground duty when I was horrified to see a lad running with a razor blade in his outstretched hand. Then I saw the sun glisten on dozens of blades, held by many boys between thumb and finger. I rang the bell as I had never rung it before, and used a voice that had never previously been heard in classroom or playground. The 'break' had only just begun, and voices from the staff called out: "Oh no, it's not time yet!" I commanded – the only suitable word – everyone to stand still.

Then walking around, I collected thirty-nine blades and a big tin containing hundreds more. The boy had found it on a rubbish dump. He proudly told me that he had shown everybody how to hold the blades; he had seen how his dad held them. He had been a good teacher, for – miracle! – no child had even a scratch. It was many a day before the staff ceased to call me the 'Sergeant Major'. I never knew that I could call forth such a voice.

46. SCHOOL INSPECTOR SAYS APPLY FOR JOB AS HEAD

School inspectors were not the most welcome visitors, but when the one who came to us at Becontree turned up in this Romford school, I was delighted and wished there were more like her to give confidence and encouragement instead of bringing a sense of apprehension and fear. How good it was to talk to this woman on all aspects of education and to hear about the plans and ideas for new schools. She suggested that I should apply for a Headship in one of the new schools being built.

What sort of Head would I have made if I had been continuing to teach? I tried to answer the question honestly, but I wasn't sure of the answer. I did know, at any rate, that I should not be so happy. I suppose that to become a Head, especially in a big school, is a sign of success in your career, but do all who aim at a headship face up to the very different life it offers? You may, of course, prefer the work it brings to teaching. I have, however, known teachers who, having accepted a headship, have sorely missed the reward they had found in the classroom.

For most of my teaching life, I taught the top class in the Infants'. At the end of the school year, these children would be from seven to eight-years old. To read some accounts of school life in the not too distant past, one is left with the impression that the system was one of constant cramming and repressive discipline. In some cases, this may have been so. But it certainly was not in the 1920s in the schools I knew.

It was not all work, work, work, sitting at a desk. One period every morning was given to Reading, one to Arithmetic, and one to Writing and Composition. These periods were for twenty minutes. In that time the teacher worked jolly hard. The atmosphere was cheerful – never any tears. Some youngsters forged ahead, others needed more help and they got it. The syllabus for the rest of the day included History and Geography stories, Scripture every morning, Singing, Games, Nature talks, Physical Exercise, and Handwork every day. There was plenty of freedom and variety, but in the time given to the three Rs, the children did give their full attention.

The boys and girls in the top class would begin in the Senior School after the summer holiday. By this time, they were expected to read reasonably well, to write a simple composition, knowing how to spell familiar words, and to have a working understanding of the three rules of Arithmetic – adding, subtraction and division in units, tens and hundreds.

Time spent with rulers in measuring every conceivable thing in the classroom, and with liquid measures and weights was much enjoyed. I cannot, indeed, stress too strongly the fact that the children were always cheerful and enthusiastic. They hated staying away from school, only sickness kept them at home. The truancy of which we hear today was quite unknown.

47. REFLECTION: LET'S PLAY FAIR NOW

Any new educational cult needs time in which to prove its worth or failure. Surely today's bias of the Play Way has been tested long enough. Many children after ten years of schooling face life retarded in the basic 'academic' skills. I fail to see what satisfaction any teacher can find in her work when pupils pass out of school unable to read, spell or write legibly, or, indeed, to speak correctly. The Play Way for the very young is one thing, but to continue this method too long is not to give our children a fair chance in life.

Far too many boys and girls pass through Primary and into Secondary School ill prepared for the work ahead and unable to reap the benefit of more advanced lessons. The system may suit a minority of children, especially when parents are intelligently concerned for their progress. What do we expect children of fifteen to do when they leave schools unable to read or who lack other basic accomplishments?

May not illiteracy play its part in producing delinquents? A boy who leaves school unable to read stands small chance of getting a good job: his opportunities are necessarily limited. Thus he may become jealous of his better-equipped rivals, and, determined not to have less money than they, may be tempted to steal. Is it mere co-incidence that we often hear that a man wanted for crime cannot read or write?

Now classes are being held throughout Britain to teach late teenagers and those up to twenty-five-years to read. More than half of the illiterates who attend these classes have normal or above normal intelligence. Yet after ten years' schooling they have never been disciplined to settle down to work. The majority of adult illiterates will not attend these classes, they have feelings of guilt and embarrassment. Talk to anyone who has left school unable to read and you will find a very unhappy youth. He desperately needs help, but a sense of shame may make him refuse it. A happy child does not grow from anti-social conduct, bred through indiscipline, fostered from early years in so-called 'progressive' schools. Self-control is necessary in any civilized society.

No educational system should be sacrosanct. Without experiment vitality cannot be maintained. There may be a few independent schools with selected pupils and not too many of them, and with an equally picked staff, in which the 'free' system is successful. But as the only or main method of teaching it is plainly less well suited to State schools with their large classes and with many of the teachers not specially equipped.

But even here there should be room for partial Play Way. Why must the pendulum forever swing from one extreme to the other? Should there not be room in any syllabus for both 'set' lessons and for 'free' periods? Discipline and freedom should not be strangers in any classroom. They are not antithetical but complementary. Let's play fair.

Half-a-century ago, I left Training College feeling that far too little attention had been focused on vocational training as distinct from theory. Reports suggest that things haven't greatly changed. Students in our Colleges of Education are given inadequate instruction. Happily the whole subject of education is again being widely re-examined, and I strongly agree with those who contend that if equal resources cannot be found for both primary and for higher education, primary schools should have the priority, since we can only build surely and effectively from the base upward.

Am I prejudiced in thinking these lines called *Infant Teacher* express the truth?

Although she wields more power
Than most who snatch the headlines of the hour,
She works remote from public view,
Her major prize

A growing confidence in the eyes
Of those who soon, forgetting her, must pass
Through higher class and class,
When others, seeing results, may claim their own
What she has sown.
Well, to the harvesters be just due.
Only: remember, now the sheaves appear,
Someone encouraged blade and ear[1].

However successful or otherwise I myself may have been as an Infant Teacher, at least I never failed to enjoy my work or lost faith in it.

In the 1920s, marriage was still a full-time occupation. But, happy as might be the prospect ahead, it was not without regret that I shut the classroom door for the last time.

---

1 This poem was written in 1963 by Dorothy's husband, Gilbert. It shows an understanding of the Infant Teacher's role, but I never remember him affirming Dorothy personally for having been an Infant Teacher. The poem was published in *Collected Poems* by Gilbert Thomas [David & Charles/ Allen & Unwin. 1969].

48. FRAGMENTS

Here are three fragments of Dorothy's autobiographical writing that were also found. The first is about her collection of pink lustre. The second, Back to the Classroom, was written after Dorothy returned to the classroom in her mid-70s as a voluntary helper (more of this in Part 3). The last is a poem.

Pink Lustre

It all began on my seventh birthday. I had been given some large tubes of various coloured paints and I didn't know where to keep them.

"I know," said my mother and went to the china cupboard. She brought out a mug saying that it had been her father's shaving mug: "Take care of it."

The mug was rather chipped, and had a lot of printing on it. My eyes saw a wide deep pink band around the top of the mug. It was my first introduction to old pink lustre and I fell in love with it at once.

That old mug was the first in a collection made in over half-a-century. I soon knew the words by heart, but I wasn't too sure of their meaning. They read:

Come my Old Friend
*   And take a pot.*
But mark now what I say,
While that thou drinkst thy
*   neighbours health,*
Drink not thine own away;
It but too often is the case

While we sit oe'r a pot
We kindly wish our Friends
  Good health
Our own is quite forgot.

I could never pass an antique shop without looking in the window to see if there were any pink lustre pieces on show. Later, I added copper lustre to the collection and some silver and the rather rare silver and blue.

Whenever you visited a small town or even a sizeable village, you could be sure of one, if not more antique shops. It might not be a smart shop but one of those delightful old junk shops. Alas, where have they gone to, or most of them? To prowl round one of these shops gave me great pleasure. They were crammed with curios and odd pieces of china, in fact anything that the owner could pick up. Much was of little worth but occasionally you would find a good piece of china. I bought a number of lustre plates, jugs and mugs this way and never paid more than a shilling or two for them.

Whenever my husband and I went on holiday, we would look around for a new piece to add to the collection.

Especially in days when we had big coal fires, in a dark room the firelight reflected in the lustre. You could go on an armchair journey. It was pleasant to let your eyes wander around the room and re-visit in imagination the places where the china had been bought.

Many of these lustre pieces were given by sailors to their sweethearts when they went to sea for long periods. Some have compasses on them and other nautical instruments. Some have very touching words for the lover to read when her sailor was far away. I loved the jug with a large circle of ribbon tied in a true lover's knot depicted on it. In the middle of the circle was the verse:

When this you see remember me
And keep me in your mind.
Let all the world say what it will
Speak of me as you find.

Biblical texts and faces of well-known divinities are on some plates and plaques. Short homilies appear on others.

So the collection of mugs, jugs, plates and many cups and saucers grew and grew. I even had a matching half-dozen small mugs for a bridesmaid's present instead of the usual jewellery.

But the time came when we were to move into a smaller house. There would not be room for all the china. We chose some favourite pieces to keep and asked an antique dealer to come to the house. I felt quite guilty when he offered prices for some jugs from £5 - £12. I knew years ago they cost me a shilling or two. I felt rather a traitor in parting with old friends.

I would have no interest in collecting anything solely because it might gain in price. My only wish to collect would be for the love of the thing itself.

Four days after the antique man had departed, I had a letter to say a friend[1] had left me a pink lustre tea service in his Will. I knew he had bought the service in Baker Street. It was perfect without a crack or blemish. When it was unpacked, I thought it was the loveliest lustre I had ever seen. What were we to do with it? No, we could not part with it. So it rests in its beauty in an old oak corner cupboard.

---

1   This was Ormond Harris. Ormond met Dorothy's husband, Gilbert, in Wormwood Scrubs prison: both as Conscientious Objectors in the First World War. They became lifelong friends until Ormond's death in the 1960s.

The old chipped shaving mug (it always has a plant in) stands nearby on my desk. It need not feel inferior for that mug began my collection[2].

Back to the Classroom

At the time of marriage, even had I wished to, I could not have continued to teach. Very few Education Authorities would have married women.

While I have always remained very interested in children and had children of my own, I had never stood in front of a class for nearly fifty years. Then I came to live near a small Primary School[3]. As I sat looking over the garden to the children playing in their field, I had a great longing to go into that school. I hesitated for a long time.

Then I went to see the Head and told her how I should love small groups of children and help them with their reading. Immediately, she welcomed me and for four years, until I left the district, I spent happy hours every week with the children. I had small groups who stayed for about twenty minutes and then the next group would arrive at the door to take their turn. I think the children enjoyed the time as much as I did.

These children were so much better dressed than the children I taught in the 1920s, and they had many more changes of clothes. What did surprise me was the interest the boys took in their clothes.

One morning, after the bell had gone I stayed on talking to the children. Then I said I must be going. "Stay a bit longer," said one

---

2   After Dorothy's death, I gave my brother, David, the pink lustre tea service and I kept the remaining odd pieces from Dorothy's collection, including the old mug. I did not know that it had belonged to Dorothy's maternal grandfather and had started her collection.
3   Chilwell Grove County Infant School, Beeston, Nottingham.

boy. When I told him that my husband would be expecting me home, he looked at me with utter astonishment.

"I didn't know old ladies had husbands," he said. That was the only time a girl or boy spoke of me as being old or any member of the staff from whom I received nothing but kindness.

I was sorry to say goodbye to a happy school that worked hard and had plenty of play.

Rooks

Do not think the law is binding,
  Or hope to reap what you have sown.
The black squadrons come a-raiding,
  And what you have is not your own.

I grew walnuts in my garden.
  The laden boughs were fair to see.
Once again the harvest's stolen:
  Not a kernel left for me.

[There was a walnut tree in the Leigh Bank garden in Teignmouth]

PART 3

DOROTHY'S STORY FROM 1928-81

by Ruth I Johns, Dorothy's daughter

Gilbert and Dorothy snapped by a street photographer in London 1928

49. MARRIAGE TO GILBERT THOMAS

Gilbert and Dorothy married at the Wesleyan Methodist Church, Rampart Road, Hythe, on August 25th 1928. Gilbert was thirty-seven and Dorothy twenty-eight.

Dorothy appears only briefly in Gilbert's autobiography[1], although it includes the first thirteen years of their married life. There is no mention of her having to leave teaching upon marriage because of the Marriage Bar or, indeed, of her teaching years at Hythe, Becontree and Romford.

Gilbert refers to the fact that he met Dorothy in the home of the Revd. Leonard Shutter at Romford, Essex. This is where Dorothy lodged when she started teaching in Becontree. Dorothy knew Leonard and his wife well because they had been in Folkestone, Kent, for some years. Dorothy grew fond of their young son, Tony, who had severe diabetes. Gilbert knew Leonard because, as Methodist Minister for Romford, he also looked after the new Gidea Park Methodist Church, where Gilbert's father attended. For a while, Gilbert played the organ for services.

In 1924, Gilbert's parents moved to Gidea Park, Essex, from Leicester, after his father retired from day-to-day involvement in their men's outfitters shops. They wanted to be near their daughter, Dora, who had health problems and to provide a home for Gilbert. He lived at home again until he married at thirty-seven. At that time his father was already terminally ill.

Of his getting to know Dorothy, Gilbert wrote in his *Autobiography*: "That this 'fair daughter of the gods, divinely tall' – she was nine years younger than myself – was keen on games and swimming would not, of itself, have tended to fire my ardour! What attracted

---

[1] *Autobiography 1891-1941* by Gilbert O Thomas [Allen & Unwin. 1946].

Dorothy 1931. Here, her hair is crimped. This was the last photo of Dorothy without permed hair. Soon after her marriage, she started having her hair permanently waved. From around the age of eleven, I was expected to have my hair permed. Having permed – as opposed to straight – hair was regarded as part of 'being ladylike'. Having hair permanently waved was a long, uncomfortable process which had to be done every four months or so

.

me was the co-existence with the sporting and eminently practical qualities, with the sense of humour and the joie-de-vivre, of a spiritual sensitiveness, a human sympathy, expressed as unmistakably in the voice as in the eyes. In her ancestry Danish pirates met English Quakers. Ours was not quite a case of love at first sight; but affection, based on a mutual understanding so solid that it could afford to be frank, developed quickly: and it has been growing ever since."

Gilbert and Dorothy set up home near to his sister Dora and within a mile of his parents. Gilbert continued to care for his parents in their last years and recognised: "My wife's position was not an easy one; but her understanding and patience did not fail."

After she married, Gilbert requested that she should no longer swim or play tennis as these were unladylike hobbies.

Gilbert held a view of marriage that was not rooted in his own early experiences. His mother had known extreme hardship in her own growing-up years and she became a hard-working live-in shop assistant. His parents met in their late twenties when both were then, in their respective departments, head assistants in an outfitters and drapery establishment. After they married, it was Gilbert's mother who suggested they get a shop of their own and she was a 'driving force' when they did so. They progressed to run a small chain of shops in Midland cities.

Gilbert (as told in his *Autobiography*) loved being a young child living over the family shop in busy Northampton Square in central Leicester. He, the youngest of three children, had a working mother until the family prospered materially. They moved first to inner suburb then to an outer leafy suburb: moves not entirely welcomed by Gilbert at the time.

But, nevertheless, on life's journey he acquired prevailing non-conformist Middle Class attitudes to marriage, including that of the role of wife. Despite having a strong character, Dorothy folded into the role set before her: nothing in her interesting life so far had prepared her for the culture shock in her life after marriage. But she harnessed her skills because she had taken a decision on life's journey and she wasn't going to be found inept. She loved Gilbert.

She too had a non-conformist upbringing, but it was quite different from that often experienced in leafy suburbs. All her life, Dorothy spoke of the warmth of the [Wesleyan] Methodist Church in Hythe, the opportunities it gave for education 'of the broadest kind' and for social enjoyment, mutual help and community togetherness. In her home, girls were definitely regarded as individuals with differing aspirations. Her parents remained in St Leonard's Road when their material circumstances improved and they enjoyed continuity of local life.

In 1929, Dorothy gave birth to David. Gilbert's father just lived to see this grandson. Gilbert's mother lived for a further six years. After my (Ruth's) birth in 1934, Dorothy and Gilbert moved into a bigger house, 25, Meadow Way, Romford, nearer to his mother who wished to keep her independent home.

After my children were born, Dorothy told me how surprised she had been when she was expected to have both her confinements in Nursing Homes. She was expected to stay in bed for almost three weeks after giving birth, although she was very fit. The enforced rest weakened her, though she tried to walk about when 'nobody was looking'! When David was born, she was brought bottle feeds to give him and told it was not wise to breast feed. By the time I was born, she insisted she try to breast feed, which she did without any problems.

In later life, Dorothy told me how tough those years were because of the cultural differences between Gilbert's and her families. For example, it fell to her to do much of the practical work of winding up the home of her parents-in-law. Gilbert's sister Dora was not well enough, his other sister Sybil (in Leicester) had a husband and son to look after and Gilbert was working. However, though Dorothy was living nearby, she also had two young children to look after. Granny Thomas's home was full of good furniture and tasteful 'treasures' and Dorothy told me that she kept very little for their own home for fear of appearing covetous.

Gilbert's parents' house was rented out and this continued until some years after the Second World War. The rent was low and, when rents were controlled, they could not be increased even when the cost of repairs rose sharply. The house was sold well below market price to the sitting tenants. Legislation did not allow it to be placed on the open market if sitting tenants wished to purchase. In the circumstances, Dorothy and Gilbert decided to sell the house in preference to neglecting repairs or subsidising the tenants. They were in total unity that money was a servant, never a master.

I mentioned earlier that Gilbert's parents, like Dorothy's, had known hardship when young and each couple responded to improved material circumstances in very different ways.

Both Gilbert's sisters were encouraged to make 'suitable' marriages, both of which held together but had severe strains. Dorothy found their ways of life very different from that of her own birth family. The Dann sisters were put under no pressure to marry particular people. Their husbands were an extremely varied bunch and were welcomed by Martha and Robert. For example, Gilbert was in prison in the First World War as a Conscientious Objector, but Robert Dann – an Army professional – welcomed him without any kind of censure. My father would remark on occasion in his later years what a 'fair man' his father-in-law had been.

In 1937, Gilbert and Dorothy felt they could follow his dream of living in the West Country. For eight months, we four travelled the West Country with a 'driver' (Mr England) in his car. We stayed in

Dorothy and Gilbert at Weston-Super-Mare 1936 with their children David and Ruth

Mr and Mrs W J Bassett-Lowke standing with Gilbert (left). Sitting: David, Dorothy and me. Leigh Bank garden c1938

hotels as the search for Eden continued. Being very young, I remember little detail of this time. My parents would later reminisce that staying in hotels in those days was possible for less than it cost to run a house!

My only memory of that time is of the pleasure of talking to strangers as we moved around from place to place. I remember only one individually: a vibrant elderly Mrs Bird who was staying in the same hotel. We liked each other's company. When we left, she gave me a large glass ball with a ship inside, an ornament she had treasured for many years. What a thrill! It still looks at me daily.

But Dorothy and Gilbert gave up the search, headed back east and bought a house in Holly Bush Lane, Harpenden, Hertfordshire, near a Dr Barnardo's Children's Home.

However within a few months, the West Country was tugging again and they travelled westwards once more, this time to stay. They sold the Harpenden house and purchased Leigh Bank, Ferndale Road, Teignmouth. It had the requisite number of rooms to allow Gilbert to have a study, David and myself separate bedrooms, a guest room and a room for Gilbert's developing model railway. This was a billiard room, re-named the Model Railway Room, which was added to the house by a previous owner. Leigh Bank had a splendid view of the sea and the Teign estuary. A stream ran along one side of the garden. The cost of such a property then bore no relation to the income/cost ratio of such properties now.

While the travelling and moving were in progress, Gilbert – now freelance – had to continue to review books and to write to keep an income stream. Dorothy managed all the practicalities, like overseeing the builders that 'did up' Leigh Bank. She managed its furnishing and, in due course, the transformation of the garden.

When I look back at my parents' relationship, there is not the least doubt that having Dorothy as a wife was indeed a gift from the gods! In the marriage of these two from backgrounds with very different ways of doing things, there is no doubt either that Dorothy did most of the adapting. She was intellectually Gilbert's equal, and used her intellect in his cause. She read his new work aloud and discussed it, offered valuable ideas, corrected manuscripts, created book indexes, and – on many occasions – made their home welcoming to visiting editors and researchers.

Over the years, Dorothy met other authors, though Gilbert was not one to socialise much. He wrote about John Masefield [1878 – 1967] who lived in Abingdon and was Poet Laureate from 1930. Masefield regarded Dorothy with the affection of an equal and shared her love of plants.

As a self-employed author, poet, literary critic and reviewer for many years, Gilbert thought he was saving enough to keep Dorothy and himself in comfort in old age. As a young man, he was well known in literary circles, and – until the 1970s – his work continued to have considerable influence. He appeared in *Who's Who* and had an Obituary in *The Times*.

In later life, Dorothy and Gilbert were philosophical about the high inflation that affected them severely, as it did many others. But this mention of their elder years is to jump ahead of our story.

Dorothy's Polyfoto sheet. Not long before War broke out, Dorothy, David and myself had Polyfotos taken. Polyfoto Limited was a national company which stated that it had: "the only system of photography giving natural and truly characteristic portraits, since the sitter can move and converse freely whilst the 48 photographs are being taken". Far from being natural, however, one was asked in quick succession to look at different spots on the wall; or to smile, look up, down, and side to side: and in the case of children to wring their arms above their heads!

50. WARTIME IN TEIGNMOUTH

During the Second World War, Leigh Bank soon became very busy. As mentioned in an earlier chapter, Dorothy's widowed mother Martha and sister May, left Hythe to live with Dorothy and Gilbert. Evacuee children from London (two sometimes but usually only one) were billeted with us because we had the space. One child developed Chicken Pox. Dorothy heard that the child's mother was also billeted in the town and contacted her, thinking she might wish to be with her child. However, the mother said: "I might catch it" and kept her distance!

Dorothy coped with the extra demands including all washing by hand. Her mother was mainly bedridden. However, we were blessed in having running hot and cold water, a bath and three indoor toilets. One, with ornate wall tiles, was next to the Model Railway Room.

Track, buildings and rolling stock of the model railway were made by the reputable firm of W J Bassett-Lowke. Some of the buildings and track-formations were made to Gilbert's own requirements. It was a masterpiece of a model railway. Bassett-Lowke photographed it on several occasions and he became a family friend. He and his wife were invited to Leigh Bank. It was Dorothy who made sure guests felt comfortable and at home.

After the Germans captured France, Teignmouth started to be bombed in tip-and-run daytime raids designed to lower morale. The planes rushed in from the sea, dropped their bombs and were gone, usually before the air raid warning siren sounded. Dorothy's mother Martha died peacefully in November 1940, before the bombing became really bad. During a few daytime raids, she refused to leave her bed, from which she had a view over the town and of the sea.

There were soon to be night raids. Bombers flew over Teignmouth to and from major cities. Returning planes, with bombs still on

The view from Martha's upstairs window at Leigh Bank. The promontory is called the Ness and is on the Shaldon side of the river Teign

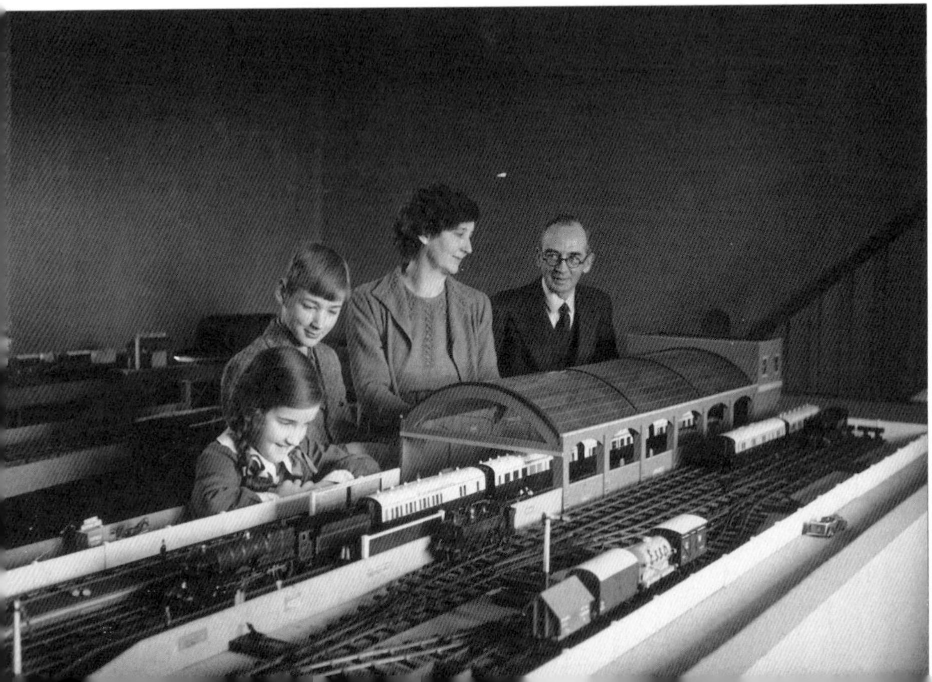

Mr W J Bassett-Lowke took this photo c1941 of Gilbert's model railway with Dorothy, Gilbert, David and me: more about the model railway later. Bassett-Lowke, from Northampton, was a model railway specialist and manufacturer who took personal interest in Gilbert's model railway

board, would circle round and round dropping their load strategically. Thus, one night in 1941, Teignmouth Hospital was hit. We spent many nights in the cellar. If adults felt fearful, they never showed it. As children do, I accepted that what happened was normal. My only fear was that one or two of us might be killed in an air raid when, during the day, we were all in different places: rather than all being killed together!

Dorothy kept a letter David had written to her in the cellar one night. It was Christmas time and he said: "My dear Mummy, I hope you have a very merry Christmas. Christmas once more has come and we will try to make it a very happy one . . . Hitler is not going to spoil our Christmas is he? . . . Well, let us forget about the War."

During long hours in the cellar, a neighbour who was an ARP [Air Raid Precaution] Warden would come through the Leigh Bank garden and knock on the cellar door and call out: "All right down there?" Because the house was built on a hill, the cellar had a door at garden level. I always worried when Gilbert went upstairs to make hot drinks before the All Clear sounded.

Looking from Leigh Bank over the town after a daytime raid was to see the whole area buried under a long-lasting cloud of thick smoke and dust. Gradually people came up from the town and passed on names of any casualties.

But, as it has to, 'normal' life continued. David and I went to school: he to the Grammar School, I to an infant school in a private house and then the local Convent of Notre Dame. Most days, Dorothy walked over a mile to town to shop for rations and other necessities when available. She did all the cooking and Leigh Bank became a food production unit. Dorothy produced vegetables and fruit in the garden and we kept chickens (we ate the eggs but could never kill the chickens, and gave them away). The Rhode Island Red chickens lived in the car-less wooden garage. A wooden ramp gave them access to a large netted pen on a lower level.

Leigh Bank, showing cellar door facing the garden whereas much of the cellar was below ground

Top of Parson Street, Teignmouth, bombed on 2nd July 1942 and near the home of Mr and Mrs Bowden who were bombed out. Photo from Teignmouth at War 1939 – 1945 written and published by Viv Wilson 2000 [ISBN 0 9539523 0 4]

During one tip-and-run air raid, Leigh Bank's chimneys were 'strafed' by machine-gun fire from a low-flying plane swooping down toward the town. It was flying only a few feet above the house. David saw the swastikas and yelled for me to lie down where I was in the garden.

Every morning early, Dorothy would walk around the garden. Years later I learned that she was checking that no German had parachute-landed overnight and, being injured, was unable to move.

Gilbert was part of the local ARP team. Its HQ was in Miss Marshall's large house on the opposite side of the road. This was just as well as my father was completely night-blind. Finding his way home, even a short way in the blackout, was difficult. Two elderly colleagues usually guided him down our gravel drive.

Before starting work in his study in the morning, Gilbert always went for a walk. When there was no school, I would often join him. We walked the narrow lanes between Teignmouth and Haldon. Sometimes, we had to scramble hastily up the steep side banks and into the hedges out of the way of tank convoys. They filled the lane totally and each tank, with its scary tracks, came upon us at speed down the hill.

Gilbert's regular domestic jobs were to mow the grass and to keep the Ideal Boiler in the kitchen stoked. It supplied heat for the kitchen and hot water for all purposes. In 1941, Gilbert's sister Dora died which meant Gilbert travelling to London for a few days. Until 1943 he sent a regular allowance to his mother's sister Emma, who died aged ninety-three in Leicestershire.

Sometimes other relatives and friends added to the household at Leigh Bank. For example, Dorothy's sister Emmeline would come for short breaks from nursing wounded soldiers. Dorothy organised morale boosting home-made concerts. Everyone present did a turn at singing, reciting or acting. The sitting room was decorated festively. There were home-made goodies to eat. But first, the blackout curtains would be checked so that no chink of light escaped. The windows were stuck with strips of sticky paper in squares, to help prevent splintered glass if the windows were broken in a raid.

We would collect whatever fruit was available locally. Dorothy would bottle some of it, and make fruit pies to eat immediately and jam and chutney to store. She discovered that it was possible to make jam with very little sugar. If there was a plum glut, we took the wheelbarrow and collected a load of fruit and pushed it a couple of miles home. For winter use, every year Dorothy sliced runner beans and salted them in large earthenware pots. These activities continued when we were evacuated and after we returned to Teignmouth.

51. EVACUATED TO SOUTH MOLTON

Teignmouth was not protected militarily and was sustaining disproportionate loss of life and damage in air raids. A directive was given that everyone who could leave the town should do so. In 1942, we evacuated at short notice, taking only clothes and family photographs, to South Molton, North Devon, as we had no overriding reason to stay. Gilbert was over fifty-years old.

Leigh Bank was offered rent-free to our half-day-a-week gardener, Mr Bowden, and his wife. They had been bombed out of their home but could not leave the town.

After a short spell at the George Hotel, South Molton, we rented a terraced house next to a garage and opposite the Police Station on South Street. We had a ringside seat of many happenings, including delivery of the extra 'rations' of meat, eggs and clotted cream to the Police Station by Exmoor farmers each Market Day! Sometimes, someone would say: "A bomb dropped ten miles away" and maybe we felt a little smug having experienced 'real' bombing. People were always surprised to learn how badly Teignmouth fared.

During the years we were away, Dorothy was very happy despite the War. Being old enough to notice, I had opportunity to experience her enjoyment of a much more easy-going informal life. We all shared a keen interest in this small market town. Dorothy continued to bring her many skills to bear on making a welcoming, interesting home: no matter that considerable improvisation was needed.

There were nearby separate camps for White and for Black American soldiers. It was our first contact with Black people beyond the occasional individual, and our first experience of racial prejudice at first hand. Most of the problems stemmed from the local population's friendship with black soldiers who were respectful. Jealousy sometimes boiled over when a local white girl

Our rented house at 65, South Street, South Molton, 1943. Gilbert, me, Dorothy and David

preferred a black boyfriend. Those involved in fights would often end up at the Police Station opposite, especially on Saturday nights.

As a young teenager over four years my senior, my brother David was in seventh heaven because he was sometimes allowed single-handedly to run the small town railway station and signal box (single-line working) whilst the signalman worked his allotment or sat chatting to friends. A 'rabbit special' train ran regularly, full of boxes of dead rabbits packed with white tails and heads showing.

At first, I was sent on the school bus from South Molton to the Preparatory department of Barnstaple Grammar School. David was at the Secondary part of the School. My school day ended earlier than the main school and I had a long wait for the school bus. So, I didn't go to school for two years. Bliss!

Dorothy taught me the three 'Rs'. We both enjoyed this. Her 'lessons' also included lots of craftwork, such as sewing, using any pieces of fabric we could find. Everything had a use. I devoured the BBC's school broadcasts and roamed the Market Town. Market Day was an education in itself. So was accompanying the local baker when he delivered bread to farms on Exmoor, or assisting the Misses Hill in their Aladdin's Cave of a Haberdashery Shop just up the road on South Street. I loved all those separate little drawers for Liberty Bodice buttons, corset bones, 'pearl' buttons and fasteners of many varieties. Almost every price was so-much plus a farthing [a quarter of an old penny, pre-decimalisation of currency in 1971].

In his spare time, Gilbert helped to sort and pack books collected for the Armed Services. Most days, he spent time sitting at the front window discussing literature and writing with a wheelchair-bound young man on the pavement outside. His wheelchair could not navigate the front door.

Dorothy and I visited the Beehive Grocery Stores regularly, where white-haired Mr Woodford served us. It was always interesting to see what was available. All local life was evident in the grocer's shop. Nobody ever seemed in a hurry. Dorothy twisted her ankle badly when walking back down South Street one day. The local doctor came and bound it up. He 'fell' for my mother and kept trying to entice her out for country spins in his car while she couldn't walk very far. He tried various tactics without success!

Our rented house was an adventure. One night the dining room ceiling fell down in large chunks. The long dark narrow hallway ran with condensation, and our garden was a tiny patch (a change from Leigh Bank's large one). But we were in the middle of everything

Back home in Leigh Bank, 1944. Gilbert and Dorothy with Mrs W J Bassett-Lowke. Leigh Bank seemed very large after the South Molton house. Note the lustre on top of the brick fireplace and on furniture. Dorothy writes about the lustre in the last chapter, Fragments, in Part 2. On the right of Dorothy is a firescreen tapestry she made. The stool has a tapestry top she made. She embroidered the chair back behind Mrs Bassett-Lowke. She made her own dress with wooden buttons that I still have

that happened. Farmers sat on the front windowsill on Market Day and their conversations (and swear words) were a treat!

Outings were usually picnics in nearby countryside, where we picked inordinate quantities of blackberries. But there were still occasional 'big' outings. Once, for example, we visited Mr and Mrs Bassett-Lowke who were staying at Woolacombe. We travelled mainly by train. The hotel menu for lunch was Tripe and Onions, or Tripe and Onions! I had never eaten this before, but was used to eating what was put in front of me. Dorothy – bless her – took pity and said I didn't have to eat the slippery but hard white stuff. When I was told what it was: no thank you!

Dorothy enjoyed nothing more than walking in the nearby countryside, knitting and sewing, reading, learning and enjoying family and friendship across the age span. It wasn't easy for her to invite her friends home because of Gilbert's work and need for quiet.

In July 1944, after the bombing stopped, it was possible to return to Teignmouth. With an odd assortment of bits and pieces we had collected, including a zinc tub full of eggs in Isinglass preservative, we travelled in the back of a van we managed to hire. Every time we went around a corner, the liquid slopped over. The family photographs were going home too.

Leigh Bank seemed enormous. Mr and Mrs Bowden greeted us affectionately and the house was in very good order. Dorothy set to and unpacked our bits and pieces and we quickly picked up Teignmouth life once more. But, South Molton had offered a human dimension that life in a big detached house on the edge of town – for me and I believe also for Dorothy – never could.

52. POST-WAR YEARS IN TEIGNMOUTH

Life was mainly good to us at this time. My brother and I were now at the same school, co-ed Teignmouth Grammar School. Soon after returning to Teignmouth, I had to sit the first ever 11-plus exam[1] and passed. Dorothy's 'lessons' in South Molton were a pleasure, and I must have been taught well.

Gilbert's work took an upturn after the War. During it, paper shortages prevented many publications. Once the War was over, Gilbert had several of his books published, including his *Autobiography*, which has been mentioned earlier in these pages.

Dorothy returned to all her Leigh Bank responsibilities. She was a brilliant self-taught gardener. She managed the large garden throughout our childhoods with little outside help. It was not only a wonderful play space but also the provenance of fresh food. She kept chickens again, stitched functionally and decoratively, providing well-mended and well-made garments and household linen, cleaned the house (with half-a-day-a-week help from Mrs. Nyus), washed everything by hand and ironed it, baked, bottled fruit, made jam and chutney, visited sick neighbours and took them food when necessary.

Dorothy was always available for David and myself, including homework queries and a welcome background presence when school friends came round. And, of course, she continued to help with Gilbert's work. Among other things, she was a first-class proof reader.

---

[1] Because I was under eleven at the time, with two other children I sat this exam even though we were already at Teignmouth Grammar School (£4 a term. Free for scholarship children). The other two 'failed' and were moved to the nearby Secondary Modern School. For me, this was an early lesson about injustice. Why should teachers and parents describe children as 'failures' because of an examination result?

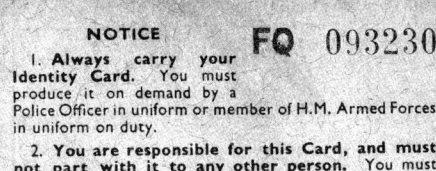

Dorothy's National Registration Identity Card

Back home, Dorothy with her children 1944

The delight of a post-war beach hut. It was used much of the year and not only on 'hot' days. Dorothy, David, Gilbert and me, 1946

The shops were over a mile's walk away again and not just up the road as at South Molton. Dorothy would have a taxi home with the heavy groceries once a week. Friends who ran cars sometimes called this extravagant, though the annual cost was less.

There was occasional but recurring tension between my parents for a few years. It had not been apparent at South Molton. Coming home from school and opening the back door, the 'atmosphere' could be palpable. My father would invite me into his study, from around the age of eleven or twelve when my mother was out at the shops or elsewhere, and confide in me. He said he probably should not do this because of my 'tender years' (and, therefore, at the time I felt very grown up).

He would always repeat the story of how, when they were engaged, he took Dorothy to see a phrenologist[2], then a fashionable thing to do. This phrenologist told him that my mother was highly strung and that, therefore, there might be times when she would be 'a little unbalanced'. I heard this over and over again. The purpose of the 'explanation' was to place responsibility for the problem on to Dorothy: I understood this only with hindsight.

My mother's explanation of the 'atmosphere' was very different. She told me not to worry, that misunderstandings happened even in the happiest of families and they did not represent any big problem. And, if I was ever worried, then I should feel free to ask questions.

Of course, I never told her about the confidences given me by my father. I had been told not to. It was many years before I allowed myself to affirm to myself that my father's confidences at that time were 'out of order'. Dorothy always spoke well of Gilbert and, for a very long time, I could not acknowledge that – in his 'confidences' – he was deeply unjust to Dorothy (and to me).

---

2 Phrenology is the theory that the mental faculties and affections are located in distinct parts of the brain denoted by prominences on the skull [from *Cassell's New English Dictionary*. 1949].

Dorothy was an avid reader and would often read aloud to Gilbert late in the evening. She also sometimes read to the family in the early evening. Books for family reading tended to be the more 'interesting' well-known novels and, thus, I became hooked on Mrs Gaskell's *Mary Barton* at an early age.

For many years after the War, relatives and friends would come for regular free holidays of a week or fortnight each summer. Included were Dorothy's Southlands College friend, Gwen, and her two sons. Thus, there were 'visitors' for three to four months each year. Dorothy fed them on good home-cooked fare, which meant substantially more groceries to shop for and carry. She would take house guests to interesting places by public transport, they would relax on the beach or in the garden and generally enjoy five-star treatment.

Later in life, Dorothy and Gilbert said, half-humorously, that – if you lived at the seaside in those days – you were sure of people visiting you! They were united in their generosity with regard to sharing what they had.

Our family hired a beach hut for some years. Sometimes Gilbert would join us there. Dorothy would swim powerfully a long way out to sea until she was a dot. I was always relieved when she was back. Gilbert did not swim. Dorothy, when young, had obtained many lifesaving awards. As we saw in an earlier chapter, swimming was one of the pursuits Gilbert asked her to give up after their marriage. But swimming in the sea did not count!

David liked school life, except for organised games, but school seemed rather a waste of time to me. There were enjoyable sides to it: like friends. And Dorothy and Gilbert allowed me to go on the first school excursion to Europe after the War. It was to Paris in 1949.

The unfair favouritism shown by the Senior Mistress irked me greatly. Some girls were punished for things others were allowed. A couple of times in summertime, I truanted and occupied myself reading and writing in the shrubberies in the large school grounds for several hours. On one occasion I walked out of school and went home without consciously thinking ahead of the impending need to offer explanations for turning up at an unexpected time!

I was able to explain the problem and my father asked the Senior Mistress to see him and Dorothy. The School had a Headmaster, and a Senior Mistress with special responsibility for the girls. For the only time I can remember, Gilbert stood up for me vehemently and it was brilliant! But, for much of my teen years, I was to learn that my role as perceived by my father was as a wife-to-be and it was much later, when I reached my late-30s, before he began to accept that I also had useful wider skills.

I would secretly detest the attention I received in my later teen years that had nothing to do with me as a person! For example, when he visited our home, at his request I gave Joseph Braddock an article I had published in 1951 (aged seventeen) after researching the background to a local ghost story. He used much of the material in a book[3]. I was mentioned in his book for bringing the story to his notice and as: "the lovely young journalist daughter of Gilbert Thomas, the poet". Nothing about my having *done* the research for the story or, indeed, of being my mother's daughter as well! It was years later that I came to realise how these attitudes must, on many occasions, also have affected my mother. My father was deemed to be skilled and a 'good man': my mother so often taken for granted as his backdrop who (as if by magic not skill!) made all his domestic arrangements efficient, beautiful and appropriate to people's needs. How often was Gilbert complimented on his hospitality, the welcoming appearance of his home and his 'charming' wife? I once dared to ask Gilbert why he didn't show Dorothy some outward affection or praise and he told me: "It isn't necessary to *demonstrate* such things"!

---

3   *Haunted Houses* by Joseph Braddock [A Batsford Book. 1956].

With hindsight, I realise that it was hard for Dorothy to comprehend that I wanted to leave school as soon as possible i.e. after passing the School Certificate examination at age fifteen. After all, how she had prized the opportunity for education, the first generation of her family to have that privilege. The agreed compromise was that, if I left school to go to Commercial College in the mornings to learn shorthand and typing for journalism, I should study for A Levels[4] in my own time. I returned to school to sit the exams. At seventeen in 1951, I obtained A Levels in Economics, History and Geography (and a scholarship to the LSE which I declined), having already started work. I wish Dorothy had lived to see me study for a research MA at the Department of Peace Studies, Bradford University, much later in my life.

My best school friend, Rosemary Broadbear (later Piper), was to remain a lifelong friend until she died in 1994. Rosemary went forward for teacher training. Dorothy never held it against me that I opted (as did my brother) to start work instead of entering Tertiary education. Through Rosemary's and my friendship, our mothers also became close friends for life. After they lived in different places, they continued to correspond and met up whenever it was possible. After a difficult spell in her life in 1980, due to a failing marriage, Rosemary included a few reminiscences in a letter to me, including: "I can still remember that the first time I went home to your house for tea, I skipped all the way home for joy – long, long ago!"

Dorothy and Gilbert never quite managed to work out their role with regard to their children's choices of teenage girl/boyfriends! Gilbert was highly suspicious of any boyfriend I might have (and Dorothy seldom contradicted him). After I left home at nineteen and was working as a journalist, a particular boyfriend, Horace Crocker, was deemed a 'bad choice' because he was a Roman Catholic. There was an assumption that any boyfriend might turn into a husband! Yet, I knew Dorothy had at least two boyfriends (one a dentist in

---

4   A Levels had just taken the place of the Higher School Certificate examination.

Dorothy and me walking in front of the shops in Torquay and being 'caught' by E A Turner's Happy Snaps '3 doors from GPO'. Late 1940s and Dorothy bravely trying the emerging 'New Look'.

Gilbert and Dorothy with niece Margaret, one of Dorothy's sister Lily's daughters, Leigh Bank 1948

May 1948, Dorothy and family return to look at Hythe after the War. Left to right: Dorothy's sister Emmeline, Dorothy, David and me about to go for a trip on the Romney, Hythe and Dymchurch Railway. We're still happy at having ice-cream again after the War. Here, we are eating small blocks of vanilla ice-cream between wafers

Food was short for a long time after the War, so chickens were kept at Leigh Bank. They had this rather splendid ramp between a large pen on the ground and the use of half the Leigh Bank car-less garage for their 'house', 1948. Dorothy cooked their food and cared for them

Gilbert, Dorothy and David, Leigh Bank garden 1949

Dorothy and pet cat Lulu in front of the Leigh Bank porch 1950

Left to right: me, Dorothy and her sister Emmeline. Looking over Leigh Bank front gate c1950

Hythe and the other a bridge engineer who was later knighted) before she met Gilbert.

Gilbert was rather at sea when David and I started to have girl and boyfriends respectively. But, as usual, if there was any friction caused by this, it was Dorothy who picked up the flack. Things that didn't work out smoothly were 'her fault' not his. This was partly because any pleading was done with Dorothy not Gilbert, this representing – obviously with hindsight – the course of action most likely to succeed!

Yet, Dorothy and Gilbert chose co-education as an enlightened secondary educational choice (and at one stage I attended a Roman Catholic Convent Junior School). But, whenever from age fourteen I went out with a boy from school to play tennis or go to the cinema, there could be trouble back home! If I met a lad who was in the town on holiday and I did the same: no problem. Thus, for example, I played tennis and went swimming with an interesting pub owner's son from Bootle, Liverpool, who was on holiday for a fortnight. Boys at my school were not always so lucky!

Occasionally, some friendship with a boy would elicit the exclamation: "I couldn't be more surprised than if you had told us you were pregnant!" Years later, as a community historian I have heard other women tell of similar parental exclamations in the 1950s and 1960s.

And whilst David's and my teenage romances were not approved of, we were not introduced to 'likely' partners through our parents' social circle because my father was not one who socialised except on rare occasions. Anyway, the liberal side of their views would regard any such social engineering as abhorrent! So we were left to choose from people we met but our choices were suspect! Dorothy and Gilbert were liberal in their ideas but Gilbert found it hard to turn ideas into practice, yet he restrained Dorothy who – left to her own devices – was pragmatic and had sound instincts.

Whether or not to attend Teignmouth Methodist Church was another unresolved matter. Sometimes David and I were taken to church as children, then for long periods not. I think Dorothy yearned for the companionship and spirit of the Church she had known in Hythe. Probably, on her own she might have found them.

Gilbert found socialising difficult. What he needed from church life, and was prepared to offer it in terms of time and effort, and what he actually found in church life left him unsatisfied. Dorothy usually enjoyed things for what they were and sought to change them – if she felt they needed it – incrementally.

Gilbert played the organ at Teignmouth Methodist Church for spells on Sundays. But whilst he liked playing the organ and was free to use it any time he wished, he found regular Sunday services increasingly difficult to cope with. Sometimes the Men's Fellowship was held in our home. Dorothy on occasions organised the weekly Women's Meeting.

Sandy Macpherson, the BBC Theatre Organist for some years, was a longstanding close and interesting friend of Dorothy and Gilbert. Sandy gave several annual organ recitals, which my parents organised, in aid of Teignmouth Methodist Church funds. When the proceeds one year were spent on new carpet for the Manse and not – as advertised – on the Church, my parents' uncertainties about 'organised religion' were sparked anew!

Dorothy and Gilbert maintained a strong faith and remained Methodists. Gilbert often wrote on matters of faith. But the question of church-going remained a fuzzy area. They wondered whether or not they should take David and I to church as children (in order for us to have the experience) or whether to do so might turn us away from what they regarded as the 'essential matters of faith'. These did not, in their view, necessarily reside within any church. In later years, Gilbert did not go to church. Later in life and after being widowed, Dorothy attended local Methodist churches when she lived in Nottingham, Teddington and Warwick and felt at home in them.

Gilbert seemed very certain that his faith enabled him to know the answers to various issues. His views could change over time but the fact that, at any one time, he felt they were under-pinned by the Christian faith could be problematic. Whilst intellectually, he believed faith should create humility, in day-to-day decision-making his views could seem intractable and not open for discussion. He never raged or ranted. He had a quiet authority that was inflexible! But, most of the time, life went on without problems.

Problems arose when Dorothy assumed Gilbert's views were right when her inner voice was silently rebelling. For many years, she suffered bilious attacks several times a year. I believe these were due to tension. She would be violently sick once or twice and then be better. It was unpleasant and she hated it. But she made no fuss. She was seriously ill only once during my growing-up years and she had to stay in bed for some days. I cooked her 'meals suitable for invalids', which I learnt to do in school, including rolled fish with sauce. She was very impressed!

On one occasion at Leigh Bank, Mrs G J, wife of a Methodist Minister, toward the end of life made a long journey from the Channel Islands. My parents knew this couple when they lived locally. The reason for the journey was that Mrs G J wanted to apologise for the envy she had felt of my mother's personality and good looks, and for her jealous behaviour toward my mother. Mrs G J wanted to feel at peace as she approached the end of her life. Such apology takes courage.

Four-and-a-half years is a significant difference in age until upwards of twenty. So as children, David and I didn't do a lot together, except on family holidays. And we had regular family meals when we all met up. David was not gregarious and his one close school friend, John Price, sadly died young of meningitis: one day he was at school, a few days later dead.

We had family holidays at least once a year. London was a favourite venue. We usually stayed at the Great Eastern Railway Hotel at

Liverpool Street. Once soon after the War, in answer to my request, we went in a London taxi for a tour of the East End. The driver thought this request: "Most unusual, very unusual!"

Whilst in London, Gilbert and David would visit the Editors of newspapers and journals for whom Gilbert worked. Dorothy and I went exploring or shopping. In those post-war years, there were still severe shortages and searching for something a little different was a challenge. I would have enjoyed the Editors sometimes! But Gilbert very seldom recognised my vocational interests (beyond the domestic skills which I enjoyed) and this was to cause problems later in life when I embarked on certain initiatives in the workplace.

For several years while I was in my teens, we all went to Bath for the week of the annual West Country Writers' Congress. On one occasion, we were invited to the amazing Victorian home of the then elderly novelist Horace Vachell. I soon discovered that writers were neither different, nor more interesting, than anyone else. Some were pompous, others amusing, some really likeable and then there were the eccentrics. To a young person in mid-teens, it was a rich experience. We'd go to concerts, including once a year to listen to the Cathedral organ.

Among areas of unresolved decision-making between Dorothy and Gilbert was the degree to which they should be 'sociable'. Gilbert regarded going to the West Country Writers' Congress as something of a major effort on his part. It was something he really did undertake more for the family than for himself. Dorothy had a natural liking for people of all sorts. Gilbert's first requirement was solitude. He was friendly to people and could be an engaging conversationalist once fired, but – like so much of life – the terms tended to be his. For example, he was willing to show visitors his model railway as we will see below. Today, Dorothy and Gilbert maybe would each 'do their thing'! Indeed, as years went by, Dorothy gradually developed independent activities but Gilbert always liked to know exactly when she would be back.

Gilbert liked regular mealtimes: Breakfast at 8.00 a.m., coffee and biscuit mid-morning, lunch at 1.00 p.m., tea with thin slices of bread and butter and a piece of home-made cake at 4.00 p.m. and supper at 7.30 p.m. Breakfast, lunch and supper were family meals. He worked in the morning after going for a walk; the afternoons were 'off' unless work was very pressing. Tea signalled a return to work until supper-time, then a 'calming of the brain' before going to bed, which was no later than 10.30 p.m. except on special occasions.

The model railway was Gilbert and David's all-consuming hobby. Gilbert wrote about this model railway[5] and, for many years after the War, an occasional but steady stream of people would call (often unannounced) during the summer months and ask to see it. Usually, they were invited in, shown the railway and given a full working display by my father and brother. Running the model railway brought a sparkle into Gilbert's eyes like nothing else and, though he sometimes found it difficult to spare the time, he enjoyed sharing the model railway with these other enthusiasts.

Dorothy would quickly 'knock up' a Victoria sponge cake, with home-made plum jam filling, and serve elegant sandwiches, tea and cake after the visitors viewed the railway. The best tea service was used (the 'Honesty' set, because it had the flower of that name in the design) with elegant little silver tea knives. I was the, sometimes reluctant, kitchen helper. I met the visitors over tea and was always eager to hear their different accents, questions and general chat.

The demonstrations and tea were freely given and were, judged by letters received, often the highlight of the visitors' holiday week.

On one occasion, my parents were deeply moved when a young ex-soldier arrived at the door with a tattered copy of an article Gilbert had written for *Model Railway News*. It included a detailed plan of his model railway. The young man knew every point, every tiny

---

[5] *Paddington to Seagood. The Story of a Model Railway* by Gilbert Thomas [Chapman & Hall. 1947].

In front of the Crescent at Bath for the West Country Writers' Congress c1950. Left to right: me, Gilbert and Dorothy

Dorothy, me, David and Gilbert in Leigh Bank garden 1952

Sandy Macpherson gave me this signed photo of him at the BBC Theatre Organ on one of his annual visits to stay with Dorothy and Gilbert from the late 1940s

A photo taken on Teignmouth Pier by roving photographer Gordon Walker of 15, Bank Street, Teignmouth, c1951. Dorothy and me, both in dresses we made ourselves

detail of the layout and said that studying it had kept him sane on the beaches of Dunkirk whilst waiting to be rescued. The model railway had two main stations, the real Paddington and the other was the imaginary Seagood.

As years went by, I became a real companion for my mother and gradually came to understand her immense strengths. We went places and spent time together, even if only to walk along the Promenade and sea wall at Teignmouth or to the end of the Pier on a fine day; or on the ferry across the river Teign to the Ness at Shaldon. Dorothy once tried to play tennis with me, but she had not played for so long that it felt uncomfortable. We both enjoyed going to the Riviera Cinema. By the time I was fourteen, we often wore clothes we each had made for ourselves. Hems were straightened by one of us standing on a table whilst the other pinned round the skirt, now at a convenient level. Walking sticks acquired marks to denote the space between skirt hem and tabletop.

Dorothy most often wore green. It was her favourite colour. I never once remember her wearing black or any shade of plain blue. Plain blue was also never a colour she chose for interior decorating. She said it was lovely for the sky but 'cold' as a static colour. But she liked tones of green/blues and brown/blues and designs that included fuchsia colours or hints of burnt orange. Dartington Hall tweeds in tans and browns were used for skirts. Viyella fabric was a favourite for home-made warmer dresses and blouses and cotton for summer.

Not at her suggestion, I asked Gilbert to allow Dorothy a regular allowance for her own clothing and personal things. Whilst not rich, our family were comfortably off at that time. Dorothy felt restrained when shopping for a dress (or often material to make one) without knowing the bounds of what was affordable. Would Gilbert think it too dear, too cheap? Having been brought up in a large family where everything was comfortably shared, she found it difficult to ask for money for herself.

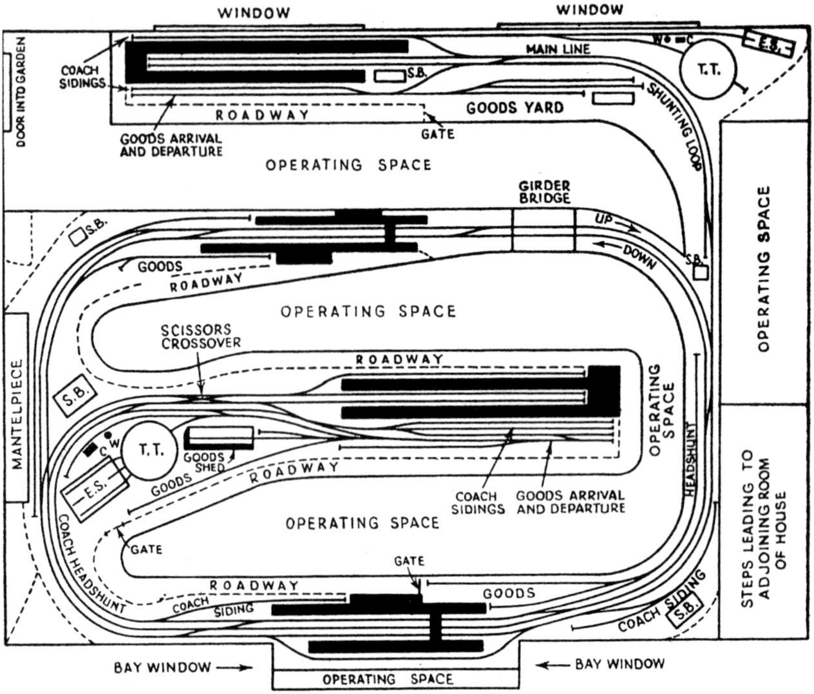

FIG. 3. Scale 6 ft. to 1 inch

This is the plan of the model railway that appeared in Model Railway News and in Gilbert's book Paddington to Seagood [Chapman & Hall. 1947]. The book was produced to the War Economy Standard: "in complete conformity with the authorised economy standards".

One of many photos of the model railway taken by W J Bassett-Lowke

Several times, she had asked Gilbert for an allowance so 'she knew where she stood'. Gilbert would say (and would tell me he had said it!): "You only have to ask and you can have anything you want." But she hated asking and he couldn't understand why. I tenaciously made a case for Dorothy having a regular personal allowance. Eventually this happened. Dorothy never spent hugely on herself but enjoyed the freedom of being able to make a spontaneous decision to buy something, even though it was usually either for the home or for someone else!

Dorothy created a beautiful home because she had a keen eye for a 'bargain' that would find its artistic or practical place around the house, and she made and mended and adapted things. One of her delights – which I grew to share – was to look round second-hand shops and markets for that something 'a little interesting'. Five shillings (25p) would be a lot to pay for something. As time went on, many of her 'tasteful bargains' would gain in value and people would say: "Oh, you could get a lot for that!" pointing to one of her treasures. This reducing of a home and its gathered artefacts to money value (or worse the thought of buying just 'for investment') appalled her[6] and, in time, cast a shadow over one of her favourite pastimes.

Dorothy was an ardent letter writer and sometimes wrote poems or essays, most of which she threw away. Her Chiropodist worked in Keats House, on The Strand in the town centre. She said the Chiropodist: ". . . ministers to my needs. I keep a rendezvous with the poet". She wrote a philosophical essay about Keats who moved to the house in March 1818 to look after his younger brother Tom, who had tuberculosis. Dorothy had a wide knowledge of literature (as, of course, did Gilbert) and she was always eager to learn for its own sake. She wasn't one to use quotations in conversation or to 'show off' knowledge. She knew dozens of poems by heart.

---

6   As she said in her Fragment on Pink Lustre in Part 2.

Teignmouth beach c1950

Teignmouth harbour c1950

I was a child of my time and not as deferential as Dorothy to my father's opinions. Her loyalties were sometimes split over things that I felt should not be an issue. For example, from my early teens I liked wearing trousers and later jeans. My father thought only 'common' women wore them. He poured scorn on Dorothy's suggestion that she would like to try wearing trousers. We saw in Part 2 that Dorothy in her past working life as a teacher could stand her ground. But in the domestic sphere she never knew how she might be allowed to agree to disagree with Gilbert.

When an issue about what I could or couldn't do as a teenager arose, Dorothy would tend to take Gilbert's opinion as her own, but not always willingly. Gilbert never changed his opinion about trousers! I wore them after the age of around sixteen and the sky never fell down! My father eventually stopped telling me he thought they didn't look nice. But Dorothy never tried them: ever.

I was forbidden to join the Yacht Club in order to learn to sail because Gilbert said there would be 'inappropriate' people there. Yet, I had total freedom to wander the town and the harbour, where I frequently – often alone – boarded the small cargo boats that berthed to unload timber and coal and to load china clay. On board, I would cook meals, collect sailors' letters to post home for them and chat about their families and countries, and talk about Teignmouth. Because my father did not have an opinion about the harbour, it escaped censure! Dorothy had a good opinion of sailors gained throughout her childhood and my experiences on cargo ships did nothing to dent it.

I hope I have not portrayed Dorothy's husband, my father, as a wilfully unkind man. He was not. He undertook his perceived role diligently. He was gifted. He was largely self-taught. Whether friends and acquaintances agreed with his views or not, most – including those in the Armed Services – recognised that he made a brave stand in the First World War as a Conscientious Objector. He had a profound knowledge of the literary world[7] and literature that made him sought after by Editors and others who valued his work. Whilst not interested in money for its own sake, he earned ample for family comfort. Our home had facilities at a time when huge sections of the population still had only outdoor toilets and a cold tap indoors.

That Gilbert was very fond of Dorothy is without question. And the feeling was reciprocated. That they became more content as they grew older was evident. But, did Gilbert ever recognise Dorothy as an independent person with enormous creative talent and humour? No!

If there were some tensions at Leigh Bank, which led to problems, there was much about home life that gave us children excellent grounding and experience. And, in hindsight, I am deeply aware how much was due to Dorothy. To be able to open your back door and jump on to a swing and swing as high as the trees for as long as you wished was a privilege. To be able to invite friends home; to have pet animals; to be able to walk just over a mile to go for a swim in the sea; to be able to walk across Haldon, or along to Sprey Point on the sea wall; to cross on the ferry to Shaldon and walk around the Ness headland; to take the train to Newton Abbot or Exeter; to sit for hours with friends in the café near the Triangle – the town's central bus stop – and watch the world go by; to go to the Cinema at least once a week; to follow the hobbies and employment of choice: these were privileges. And we knew we were loved.

Both David and I entered journalism. He started at Plymouth, living in lodgings, after serving his National Service time as a Conscientious Objector working on the land. He worked first for the *Independent* (a local weekly paper) and then in the Plymouth office of the *Western Morning News*.

I served a two-year Indenture on the weekly *Mid-Devon Advertiser* at Newton Abbot. In those days, the recommended – and often only

---

7   His works of scholarship included *William Cowper and the eighteenth century* [George Allen & Unwin Ltd. 1935. Revised second edition 1948]. This was accepted as a standard work for many years in the UK and USA.

David's wedding day 1954, Cornwood, near Plymouth. Left to right: Gilbert, Dorothy, me, David, Pamela, Jim Shepherd (Pamela's brother) and Mary and Dick Shepherd (Pamela's parents)

Dorothy (centre) among the guests, after my school friend Rosemary Broadbear's wedding in Teignmouth mid-1950s. I am the bridesmaid

– entry for journalism was to get in young and women were seldom accepted. No Media degrees then! By nineteen, I was in Exeter, a staff reporter on the *Western Morning News* and living in a rented flat at the top of a family home. Dorothy helped me to furnish it and she sometimes came up to Exeter on my day off.

I would often go home to Teignmouth in my time off. I bought a 1939 Austin Eight car and travelled proudly with my Press notice on the windscreen. On the car's second excursion, I took my parents to Torquay. They must have crossed their fingers as I drove along the winding coastal road. It had sheer drops down the cliffs near the edge of the road in places. Dorothy was always delighted to share time. Gilbert found it more problematic. I once phoned Dorothy from Exeter to say I couldn't come home as agreed because I had broken out in German Measles. She was overjoyed! At first I did not understand the reason[8].

With David and me living away from home before the mid-1950s, another phase in Dorothy and Gilbert's life was soon to begin.

---

8   Because of the risk to a foetus if a pregnant woman has German Measles [Rubella].

53. GOODBYE TO LEIGH BANK BUT STILL IN TEIGNMOUTH

With children 'flown the nest', Leigh Bank was too big and becoming too costly to run. But, what next? Dorothy and Gilbert had no clear idea what this next stage should be.

Gilbert, now into his 60s, was still working, writing articles and poems, and reviewing books for a range of newspapers and journals. In fact, during this next phase of Dorothy and Gilbert's life, he was to start a long association as a regular reviewer for the *Birmingham Post's* weekly book page from the late 1950s until he was over eighty-years old. On September 18th 1966, when he was seventy-five, his long poem *One Man's Tribute*, spoken by himself and Rex Palmer, was broadcast as one of the BBC's Evening Worship Series. It took half-an-hour: an unusually long time for a broadcast poem. But this is to jump ahead of the story.

And Dorothy? She saw less point managing a large house now, though friends and relatives still came to stay. I once suggested she might think about returning to teaching, part-time. She liked the idea. But the practicalities of changing the routine of their lives to encompass such a change were not something Gilbert could envisage. And, Dorothy's personal confidence was not high at this time, though she could accomplish much in other's causes. Dorothy regularly read Gilbert's articles and reviews for 'typos' before they were posted. She offered helpful revisions when sometimes shown a draft for comment.

In April 1953, a letter from Gilbert to me was written just before Dorothy and he were setting off for a London holiday. He says Dorothy's sister Emmeline would spend a night with them at the Ivanhoe Hotel before she and Dorothy visited Woodford (to see their sister Lily) the next day.

Most of this letter from him was reporting 'between ourselves' how Dorothy had been: "very much and nicely opening her heart to me

Dorothy and Gilbert glad to be back in Teignmouth! Sitting on the Den 1955

Yannon Tower 1955. Dorothy and Gilbert rented the first-floor flat

Home for a weekend, me with Dorothy on Teignmouth beach 1955

about David. I was busy during the weekend, but I gather she was much hurt by his curt and over-riding behaviour, and his apparent lack of interest in ourselves and our holiday – all of which, she says, could not be excused on the ground that he was tired. He certainly does too much and does get over-tired, but Mummy says she is determined as never before that he must learn that we can no longer 100% carry him. It is a pity that, being such a good fellow in many ways, he seems to lack the flower of imagination and courtesy sometimes".

I include the above as an example of how Gilbert tended to express his own feelings through Dorothy's actual or assumed words. I have no idea, of course, what exactly Dorothy may have said on that particular occasion, but I am sure that she never intended it to be seriously reported 'between ourselves' to me with Gilbert's added comments to give it weight. And why did Gilbert say she 'was nicely opening her heart' to him? What individual does not sometimes 'sound off' to a loved one? In later years, there were to be other occasions when such thoughts were imprisoned in letters to me about David, and – at one point – I know about me to him and indeed to a range of others, including Keith Brace, Literary Editor of the *Birmingham Post*!

My parents sold Leigh Bank and, at first, thought of moving to Torquay and for a brief time in 1954 stayed at the Elmington Hotel, St Agnes Lane, Torquay. They intended to rent a flat to see how life developed, but Gilbert wrote to me in March 1954: "We have practically decided that we will continue to live in Teignmouth! I think it was wise to come here, if only to appreciate the advantages of Teignmouth!"

They rented the middle flat in Yannon Tower, on Exeter Road, Teignmouth. This large building was a folly built in pleasant grounds and overlooking the river Teign and the sea. Their idea was to test whether they liked renting with no property maintenance responsibilities. Having more time to do things together was appealing. The flat was pleasant, far fewer rooms but spacious ones. There was space for guests and David and myself for home visits. A painter and decorator painted the walls of the flat and Dorothy painted all the gloss work (windows, skirting boards and doors) throughout.

The move from Leigh Bank meant selling the model railway. That was sad but, also, liberating. The effort of people visiting it was getting harder as the years rolled on, and Dorothy and Gilbert didn't like to say 'no' to people wishing to see it working.

Around this time, I first realised how much both my parents represented the history of their particular times and previous life circumstances as well as having their own distinct personalities. Maybe this is what set me on a long journey that ended up with becoming a community historian. Here was Dorothy, gutsy, fun-loving, serious, rock-solid values, kind and empathetic to relatives, friends and strangers: yet nothing in her life had prepared her for this situation. Her own parents had simply stayed in their modest home in the heart of Hythe and life went on. It was busy with family comings and goings and local commitments. That is what Dorothy would have liked, to be part of life that went on but on a manageable scale. At the time, I didn't have the maturity fully to see what was happening.

Gilbert stated openly that he would do anything Dorothy wished, full knowing she would do as he wished! And he sought an ordered, quiet life, so he could accomplish his work, with an empathetic partner who managed a tranquil spacious home and almost all domestic matters.

Whilst they were at Yannon Tower, I helped to persuade Gilbert to allow Dorothy to take driving lessons after she mentioned it several times. She enjoyed the new challenge. At age fifty-six, she passed her driving test at the second attempt. Gilbert bought a car and Dorothy drove until she was seventy-five. In those years, they both travelled all over the country together for short breaks, and it gave them much pleasure.

Dorothy, as ever, did most of the practical work and all the driving, adding chauffeur to her skills, but she enjoyed it. Over the years, they had two cars in succession, first a second-hand Triumph and later a new Morris Cowley. The Morris had a front bench seat and the gear stick was on the steering column. I drove this car sometimes and it felt like a small tank!

They picnicked in places, usually with a sea or river view, around Teignmouth whenever the weather was fine. They had a particular spot at Powderham that was a favourite. Picnics usually consisted of sandwiches and cake, and a thermos of tea, for afternoon tea.

It was around this time that Dorothy started to drink tea, always having preferred hot water. As she grew older, people assumed that drinking hot water was not a matter of choice but a health issue. Finally fed up with being asked if she suffered from indigestion, she started to drink *very* weak tea without milk or sugar but, if possible, with a couple of thin slices of lemon.

Dorothy missed having a garden and not being able to 'step out of a back door on to the earth'. Gilbert felt somewhat trapped by needing to walk on the busy pavement-less Exeter Road before getting anywhere. He still undertook regular 'constitutional' walks morning and later in the day, though they were much shorter walks than in earlier times.

The next project soon began. It was to plan their new house, which would be much smaller than Leigh Bank but big enough to enable guests to stay. They bought a plot of land on nearby Yannon Drive. Dorothy spent happy weeks helping to design and plan their new home: Hesper, Yannon Drive, Teignmouth. In fact its front gate was on Yannon Drive and its back gate on Higher Yannon Drive, which afforded a useful choice of walking routes.

A reputable local builder built the house. After moving in, Dorothy's challenge was a virgin garden. She had outside help with laying the lawn and some of the early heavy work. Within two years, the garden was a picture.

Dorothy's grandson Martin in his pram, Hesper back garden overlooking the river Teign, 1958. And Hesper front view which overlooked the sea, 1958. The garden was still very new as shown by two young trees

Dorothy with grandchildren Martin and Alison [now Alyss] when they decided to kiss each other, 1959

Dorothy and Gilbert came to Oxford just after the birth of Martin, my first child, in 1958. I was married and we lived at 85, Southmoor Road, backing on to a canal, railway and Port Meadow beyond. We had a small attic flat with a cold tap and stone sink, and shared bathroom on the floor below. There was no room for guests. My parents stayed at a nearby guesthouse for over a week. Having promised them that we would not marry until he had his degree, my first husband – a post-National Service student – persuaded me of his need to have me near. So we married quietly in Oxford in 1956. And I gave up journalism because its hours were too erratic for his comfort. Giving up journalism at that time was a big mistake. Oh, how history can repeat itself in different circumstances!

Husband, a few-months-old Martin and I left Oxford and stayed at the newly built Hesper in Teignmouth for six weeks before moving to 4, Oxhill Road, Handsworth, Birmingham, where we rented two rooms plus box room in the home of an elderly widow, Mrs Garrett. After Gilbert and Dorothy visited us in Birmingham, Dorothy wrote: "Daddy is not one to come too easily to anchor outside his own walls, but I know how contented he was . . . Mrs Garrett is a very unusual woman . . . You are lucky . . . We miss choral song from Martin. He is a dear soul. We have two lovely grandchildren. I was glad to see the park [Handsworth Park] for you to have a good place to stretch your legs. I thought the air was good, much better than I thought it would be."

For some years to come, it was to Hesper, Teignmouth, that Martin and later my other children came with me for several weeks each year as well as many of our family holidays. They loved these times. Before we owned a car, we would make the journey by train or, occasionally if we were all going, in a rented car.

My brother David and his wife Pamela were also building a family, living first in Kingskerswell and then at Bittons, Ipplepen, in Devon. His daughter Alison [now Alyss] was born a year before Martin. She was blonde and Martin very dark. Dorothy sometimes took us all to Madge Mellors's café in Newton Abbot for a treat. On one occasion,

*Martin, me,
Dorothy and
Gilbert, Bolton
Abbey 1959*

*At 59, Hartley
Street, Rochdale.
Gilbert and
Dorothy with
Martin*

*Dorothy and Gilbert visiting us
at Lichfield, May 1961. Seen
here with Martin and Naomi*

230

Dorothy and I were with the two children. Someone on the next table assumed both children were mine and commented: "I expect the father is blond!' How easily are assumptions made!

In 1960, my daughter Naomi was born. By then, we were living in Rochdale, first in a rented house in Bowness Avenue and then in our first owned house, a small semi-detached one at 59, Hartley Street, Rochdale, where Naomi was born at home. Dorothy motored from Teignmouth to Rochdale on her own, mostly in dreadful weather, to help after Naomi's birth. To be looked after, Gilbert went to stay with David and Pamela. This separation was a new venture for Dorothy. Gilbert allowed it, but his letters to Dorothy whilst she was away left her in no doubt that he would be pleased to have her back. His letters began: "Dear Doggie eyes", "dear old Doggie-eyes," or "My dearest Doggie". Dorothy called him Gilbie at the start of letters.

After her death, I saw and treasured letters written by Gilbert to Dorothy at such times. They expressed a warmth that I never saw him express openly. For example, he wrote: "Fondest love to all, and a very special portion for your dear self. 'I thank God on every remembrance of you'. Who said that? Anyway, I do! Ever your own Gilbert."

In one of her letters to me around this time, Dorothy wrote: "Daddy and I keep bursting out laughing at the thought of both being on the Third Programme together [following an interview]. I bet my last penny that not a word I said will be used and they will only cut a sentence from Daddy here or there. All most unsatisfactory." So Dorothy was, without any bitterness, very aware of the ways of the world!

After her birth, Naomi soon succumbed to congested lungs (Rochdale in 1960 had very polluted air). Our doctor, Dr Portnoy, said he would normally suggest she went to hospital, but the best care would be at home if we could burn the coal fire all night and keep her upright. Dorothy came up to help. All night while Dorothy slept, I sat up cradling Naomi so she was never lying flat. Then in the daytime, when Naomi could breathe more easily, Dorothy looked after her and Martin whilst I slept in the mornings. When Naomi was sleeping in the sitting room during the day, Dorothy placed an umbrella stand outside its door in the hall. Martin, still under two-years, knew this meant he should not enter because his new sister was asleep. She slept very fitfully.

There was an old greenhouse in the garden. Dorothy and I created a play area Martin adored: lots of small pots, earth, seeds and plants which he potted and planted and re-planted, and emptied out and started again. No matter that some of the plants were garden weeds. To keep his interest, there were pots of different sizes and a small jug that had to be filled often in order to water them. And then the greenhouse itself had to be tidied, decorated to make the planted pots look good . . .

On that visit, Dorothy stayed longer than she intended due to the circumstances. Some months later, Naomi was ill again and we took her down to Teignmouth for the fresh clean sea air. Martin, Naomi and I stayed for some weeks. Once again, Dorothy to the rescue.

Both Dorothy and Gilbert visited Rochdale several times while we were there and they liked it. Gilbert wrote about it. Our house was small, so my parents stayed in the centre of the town in a pub hotel. Years before, Gilbert would not have countenanced staying in such a 'hub'. As he grew older, he himself grew quieter and did not 'chatter' like most of us. But he seemed more to enjoy being amongst the chatter, providing he could be quiet.

Another move beckoned, due to my husband's work moving to Birmingham. Dorothy and Gilbert stayed in a guesthouse in the Birmingham area (I cannot remember where exactly) and I came down from Rochdale with the children to join them in order to house-hunt. The memory lingers of having to make up Naomi's bottle in the guesthouse kitchen, which was very grubby. No point in complaining: there were few places available to stay. Dorothy drove us round to look at houses. One in Lichfield was chosen.

Neil was born at home at 97, Valley Lane, Lichfield, in 1961. Dorothy arrived a few hours before I went into labour. Late in the evening the midwife said she thought nothing would happen for some hours and she intended to leave for a while. Dorothy knew I thought 'things' were imminent, so she offered to do the midwife's knitting, which she was advancing lethargically. Dorothy, being a rapid, even knitter, took over the knitting project – the last long sleeve of a jumper – and the midwife sat back, relaxed with a cup of tea and watched with great pleasure. Neil was indeed imminent and was born just after Midnight. By the time the midwife had attended to everything and tidied up, her knitting was complete! The midwife was amazed how neatly Dorothy had stitched the jumper together and pressed it.

Neither Dorothy nor my husband was present at the birth of any of my children. A few husbands at that time were present when their babies were born, and, of course, today often a female relative or friend is. When Dorothy's mother Martha gave birth, her mother (Mary Ann) was usually present. It seems that when people begin to get better off materially, some sound human interactions are often lost in favour of 'newer and advanced' ways of doing things. Then, years later, the good part of traditional culture – like not having to give birth alone with only a professional helper – reasserts itself as if it were a totally new concept!

There were no other children near where we lived at that time. I started a playgroup three mornings a week so that Martin in particular had experience of playing with other children, and in order to help us to put down roots. Dorothy and Gilbert came up for visits. Dorothy found a second-hand china shop in Lichfield where she and I purchased some useful pieces. Some I still use regularly.

During these years, Dorothy was also involved with my brother's family who lived only half-an-hour away from Teignmouth. The year after Neil was born, I was very ill (with a muscle problem that had arisen briefly when I was twenty and was to recur seriously in 1984). My husband drove our three children and me from Lichfield down to Teignmouth where, for six weeks, Dorothy looked after us

Naomi and Martin's awe at the space on Teignmouth beach on the first day of our early summer stay 1961. Seen here with Dorothy, as usual wearing a dress and jacket she made herself

Dorothy with grandchildren Martin, Neil (on lap) and Naomi whilst I was visiting Teignmouth with them. Taken at Torquay 1963

Dorothy with Neil and Naomi on the roof rack of our hired car for holiday to Teignmouth. On Haldon, summer 1964

Dorothy and Gilbert in Hesper garden 1965

single-handed. I was too weak to do anything for these weeks, and then slowly recovered.

At that time Dorothy was sixty-two. She was desperately worried about me and I learned afterwards that, at one time, she feared for my life. Gilbert spent much of the day in his study. He was still working part-time. He was seventy-one then, and though he didn't mind us all in the house, he didn't take part in much that happened with the children. The three of them were under five. He loved them dearly in his own way and they him. It wasn't until I became the age Dorothy was then that I fully realised the extent of what she undertook with skill, love and generosity for us all at that time. Without her, the children might well have gone temporarily 'into care'.

Years later, after Dorothy died, my then husband wrote: "She was a very kind-hearted person and good to us in many ways when the children were small."

Soon we were on the move yet again – to Nottingham. This time, Dorothy and Gilbert came and stayed with us in Lichfield. Every day for over a week, Dorothy drove the children and me over to West Bridgford, Nottingham, to house-hunt. We usually stopped en route at Attenborough Nature Reserve for the children to have a run round and to eat the picnic we brought with us. As ever, mother and daughter turning work into fun! During all these times of meeting up and helping out, Dorothy was – in different circumstances – achieving the interactive close relationships that were the hallmark of her birth family.

By late 1963, our home was at 55, Repton Road, West Bridgford. Not a happy time. Before long, the prospect of another move, to Hull or Doncaster, began to loom. For what? How long for? Why? Martin was very unhappy at the local Primary School where punishment (for example, being sent to stand alone in the cloakroom) was meted out for incorrect spellings and it was a school where parents were tolerated (only by appointment) and not welcome. Naomi later started for a short while at the same school and fared a little better.

Martin did not thrive and was taken out of school, spending mornings having home teaching with a teacher friend of mine and spending afternoons at home.

Fortunately, I enjoyed home-making in whatever circumstances life happened and I enjoyed being a mother. But, in West Bridgford, I was desperately lonely, but could also see that moving on and on – never long enough to make lasting friends – was leading nowhere.

I began to see, for some very different reasons – but also some with connections – that was how Dorothy felt. I didn't appreciate it at the time, but she and I were searching for the same thing: a life where there was a community; where people grew up and had continuing extended family and long-lasting friends. Our extended family links were strong. But being together was episodic.

Gilbert liked people but didn't need them: Dorothy did. They did not aspire to be rich as many in their strata of society did. Gilbert was content with a degree of comfort, solitude, the occasional social discourse, and the stimulus that came through his work (which still involved visits from people like Keith Brace, Literary Editor of the *Birmingham Post* and Margaret Willey of the literary journal *English)*. For him, this was enough because all the community he needed was Dorothy!

I have no illusions that yesteryear was necessarily better and that communities were necessarily closer. But there is plenty of evidence that, in childhood and as a young adult, Dorothy experienced Hythe as a close community. For people like Gilbert and Dorothy at their time in history, it seemed inevitable that Dorothy would be inwardly lonely. I explained earlier that, because of the Marriage Bar, she was denied any continuation of her teaching life after she married and she had no experience of how a married intelligent woman might live in a nuclear family in a Middle Class suburban setting other than to offer her husband, children, relatives and friends her myriad skills and affection.

236

Gilbert's mother aspired to and chose to live the Middle Class way in a suburban setting. Dorothy, on the other hand, married into the Middle Class suburban way. Friends and relatives assumed that Dorothy and Gilbert, both from Methodist families, had a similar background. Earlier, I outlined this fallacy. Often, she believed Gilbert's views on things to be correct because she shared them. But, as we have seen, even when she did not, there was little other course of action available to her. She used her talents in the life that was available to her and she used them abundantly. But, they were constrained. I wonder how Dorothy would have worked things out had she been born three or four decades later?

Dorothy, as an independent talented spirit, was never acknowledged either publicly or privately after her marriage. And I am not expounding a feminist thesis, because, in my view, feminism has left a lot of questions unanswered.

Once, Gilbert wrote a poem *For Dorothy*[1].

For Dorothy

These chores! This new domestic look!
  How much, dear heart,
    There is to do!
    Still, I am not amazed that you –
Wife, housewife, granny, gardener, chauffeur, cook –
  Compass each part,
    Taking all within your stride.
Here lies the miracle,
    Touching more than pride:
In Martha there, undimmed, can dwell
Mary as well.

---

[1] *Collected Poems* by Gilbert Thomas [David & Charles/George Allen & Unwin. 1969].

54. MOVING NORTH AND WONDERING WHERE TO SETTLE

By 1964, Dorothy and Gilbert were thinking of moving north to be nearer us. At first they thought it might be Hull. But that move (or possibly Doncaster) didn't take place. I finally found my voice and decided that our family could no longer keep moving. My husband left a large company and joined a small firm of local consultants. That didn't work out. He planned to work on his own as Triangle Personnel Services, but then joined another major company for a while before taking another job working away most weeks.

For some time I had been openly working out the practicalities of a community housing venture in Nottingham and becoming 'rooted' in one place as a family. We would have independent accommodation in a large building used for the initial project. It is not relevant to say much about the project here[1].

It is important, however, to Dorothy's story because she and Gilbert accepted that they wished to be part of it to the extent that we would be a three-generation family living on site. Dorothy and Gilbert sold Hesper. They moved up to Nottingham in 1966 and became tenants in their own flat close-by us in the converted large house. In fact, it didn't work out. Gilbert's views in particular did not accord with my ideas about how young homeless individuals (mainly young mums) and – as Family First grew – many families were accommodated in a growing number of properties. And he found it difficult to believe that I might know what I was doing!

---

1 I have written about it in *Life Goes On: Self-help philosophy and practice based on over ten years' pioneering work with the Family First Trust, Nottingham* by Ruth I Johns [1982]. I decided to publish this myself after several large publishers wanted to publish it conditional on turning it into a guru-style handbook, which I refused to do. The book received twenty-five good reviews, is still read and in print.

He also felt that my relaxed style of parenting and sharing much time with my children was 'too modern'! Dorothy, once more, found herself having to agree with him whilst finding this created tension in herself and between us. She actually loved much about the work in progress and having the grandchildren in her daily life.

Dorothy and Gilbert were – post-Lichfield – also becoming increasingly aware of difficulties in my marriage. Although they had at first thought it an unwise marriage, they had supported us wholeheartedly over the years once we were married. They never sought to undermine us.

The upshot was that Dorothy and Gilbert returned to Devon within a couple of years to live in a new bungalow in Ipplepen some half-mile from my brother. My relationship with Gilbert and Dorothy resumed its normal course. Once more, letters each week and telephone calls each week to and fro, again we were spending several weeks a year in Devon, this time using our Dormobile camping van as an extra bedroom at the side of their two-bedroom bungalow.

Dorothy and Gilbert came to us in Nottingham at least twice a year. At distance, intellectually Gilbert gradually grew to support and understand what the Nottingham project was achieving and wrote warmly of it. It was achieving much for many people, creating a secure home for our family and providing us with a warm community both through the project and in the neighbourhood.

However, at the end of 1973 my marriage broke up, my husband wanted independence and I became the family breadwinner. This caused Dorothy and Gilbert sadness but they truly surprised me with their solid uncritical and balanced understanding.

Soon after, Dorothy wrote: ". . . It is extra difficult for you when the children are at their most demanding. How I wish I knew the answer. But I'm sure you will be wise to accept what you cannot change."

Gilbert and Dorothy remained in good relationship with my ex-in-laws and they with me, especially my mother-in-law. Whilst very different from Dorothy's, her adult life bore many parallel patterns. She continued to call me 'daughter' and affirmed my being a good mother. Dorothy and she also corresponded and, occasionally, both couples met up.

Gilbert was still working part-time and life in Ipplepen was satisfactory, with a car for frequent small excursions and occasional longer ones. Dorothy found a number of congenial friends. In a letter to me, she wrote: "I don't think many men make friends like women do . . . Many women make their own social life apart from their husbands . . . To a great extent I have done this and it works well."

David and his wife, Pamela, were busy building up the publishing house of David & Charles in Newton Abbot. My elder son Martin spent a couple of enjoyable weeks (notwithstanding getting mumps) on his own with his maternal grandparents in Ipplepen. Dorothy and Gilbert at this stage of life reached a companionship that was very comfortable. Dorothy and Gilbert took a great interest in their five grandchildren (two from David and three from me). Gilbert, at over eighty, still usually wrote handwritten letters to me, often one a week. Dorothy too. Her handwriting did not improve with the years!

When they moved into the Ipplepen bungalow, which they called Woodthorpe after the park in Nottingham, Dorothy again was faced with a virgin garden and, again, she quickly created a stunning garden with colour all the year round. It was a corner plot and gave much pleasure to passers-by.

Having created two gardens from builders' rubble and the one at Leigh Bank from an unkempt wilderness, she wrote a manuscript about the enjoyment and practicalities of an amateur making a garden. This was decades before a glut of gardening books hit bookshop shelves. I read the MS and, whilst in those days my gardening skills were still embryonic, it was a good read and informative. At his request, she showed the MS to David (by then a successful publisher). He made no comment on the MS for many months. She eventually asked for it back and it was returned without comment. She destroyed it believing it was 'not very good'. She had very little self-confidence despite appearances to the contrary.

Dorothy used the car to help with Meals on Wheels and to provide transport for people to and from hospitals in Newton Abbot or Torquay. She would sometimes refer to a sermon she once heard, in which the preacher remarked that, in Heaven, people would have to do what they did best in this life. "Never" she exclaimed!

But, after a few years, two things were to spoil these times. Firstly, Dorothy – for the first time in her life – became seriously indisposed with a severe and long-lasting headache. This affected her ability to do many of the things she both needed to do and/or enjoyed doing. This frightened her because she wondered how Gilbert and she would cope if this problem continued. Secondly, there was a big flare-up between David and his father. Not my purpose here to go into that in detail but the upshot was that for the rest of Gilbert's life they were unable to resolve matters. That was particularly tough on Dorothy.

Gilbert did not acquire as much money as he could have done during his working life: a facet of his character that his son found difficult to comprehend. Gilbert would not do 'pot boil' writing. David sometimes refers to our childhood as if we were impoverished and expresses regrets that he didn't go to University, but that was not due to lack of finance. Our parents would have liked us both to go to University. David felt Gilbert did not admire his own son's success. Each had a different view of his destiny. They clashed, I believe, because in some fundamental ways they were very similar. It happens.

Perhaps in too much haste, but understandably, in 1975 Dorothy and Gilbert left Ipplepen and moved into sheltered accommodation at the Queenswood Methodist Home for the Aged at Chilwell, Nottingham. They did not own the bungalow in Ipplepen. I had a frank talk with them about the wisdom of moving. By then, it was almost certain that we would be moving from Nottingham in the not-too-distant future if I could find a suitable job in London that could pay a 100% loan and

Advertisement for the sale of Hesper 1965

Gilbert and Dorothy in the small summerhouse in their Ipplepen garden 1973

Dorothy, day out 1974

Dorothy at Hampton Court during visit to my family summer 1977

244

Dorothy was determined to be strong. She continued to help in the local school and would write to me about events like sports day. She found life in the Methodist Home on her own lonely, though she had some good friends there. The other residents were mostly women on their own. She offered all sorts of help to people, which was welcomed but she desperately needed emotional support herself. People, even her close friends, never regarded her as elderly. Indeed she would be standing up on buses offering her seat to 'elderly people' who were sometimes considerably younger than her!

She continued to feel Gilbert was: "very near me" and she would sometimes talk as if he was there. She wrote a moving poem soon after Gilbert died. I found it amongst her papers, written in long hand and she obviously hadn't 'worked' on it but left it as it came into her head.

The Fadeless Tapestry

Together
We wove the pattern of life.
When you died
The weaving ceased.
Yet, every day the big canvas
Glows with a lustre of its own.
Bright stitches put in with laughter.
Gleaming threads when the children were born.
And of the darkling clouds
Of troubled days.
Luminous moonlight on the summer seas,
And the golden harvest of the fields.
Row upon row of coloured books:
Tangled skeins we unravelled for work
In home and garden.

Dorothy, me, and my daughter Naomi on a day out in Brighton 1978

53, Broom Park, Teddington, 1979. Front row left to right: Dorothy, me, Naomi. Back row: Martin, friend Steven, and Neil

Crystal moments of understanding:
Moments out of time that sparkle
Like diamonds.
All, all are there in the fadeless tapestry.

The rows of books allude to all the books Gilbert had for review over many years. In her mind's eye, Dorothy had visualised them in 'row upon row'. In fact, of course, they were not all kept otherwise the rows would be never-ending! A bookshop in London bought review copies at half-price.

The literal skeins Gilbert and Dorothy unravelled were those that Gilbert sometimes held between his outstretched arms after supper in the evening as Dorothy rolled balls of wool for her knitting. It was not a favourite pastime of Gilbert's and he sometimes got the wool in a muddle, but they had a good laugh over it.

Dorothy soon came for a break in Teddington for a couple of weeks and visited David in Devon. I was planning to marry Walter in 1979, which would eventually mean moving to Warwick. He worked in Coventry. By then, my children would all have completed schooling and be taking a gap year, working or at University. Warwick would become a future family base.

When Naomi left home to share with a friend in nearby Twickenham, I thought and thought about the wisdom of inviting Dorothy to join my family at Teddington only for her to have to move to Warwick with us a few months later. She was looking forward to that. I asked her and she jumped at the chance and moved into 53, Broom Park on February 15th 1980, putting her own furniture temporarily into store. She had already spent much time in Teddington in the previous two years.

Dorothy then 'retired' from her voluntary help in school. Each child in her current group drew their face on a very long specially made open-up card to wish her well. Her happy return to 'work' in a school again when she was seventy-five to nearly eighty-years makes me

Dorothy stepping out of the hired Social Services van after Walter's and my wedding, November 1979. With me and Walter, and Paula (Walter's mother) in foreground

wonder what might have happened had she not been forced to give up teaching when she was twenty-eight.

We had some really good times together in Teddington, like her eightieth birthday and a picnic on Brighton beach with the three generations of 'girls': Dorothy, me and Naomi, who was exploring the world of work before gaining a first class degree in Craft, Design and Technology in her mid-twenties. Dorothy enjoyed discussing craft projects with Naomi and they shared many ideas. Neil was studying for 'A' Levels and Dorothy took an interest in his work and friends, also his job as Saturday Manager at the Men's Department of Russell & Bromley's shoe shop in Kingston upon Thames. Martin was studying at Aberystwyth University and would often be in Teddington in his vacation time.

Meal in an Italian restaurant on the evening of our wedding day. Left to right: Dorothy, Walter, me, Naomi, Neil (just!) and Paula (Walter's mother)

Dorothy at end of table: Christmas, Teddington, 1979. Naomi (left) and me and Neil (right)

When my brother came for a visit, Dorothy would instinctively say he must be tired after a hard day's work. Dorothy was brilliant at having a meal prepared for the evening, but – though she loved me to bits – she failed to relate to the fact that not only was I working but, as our family breadwinner, I *had* to work! I might be tired in her eyes, but never because I worked! For example, when I came home in the evening, I needed a short quiet spell to change gear after a day's work and the commuting journey before joining in the family chat. My children understood this.

Dorothy would go straight into chat! It was only when I discovered after her death that she had given up her teaching career because she had to, not because she chose to, that I came to understand her ambivalence about women working. Intellectually, she understood. But her own life experience, which I hope is communicated above, left her – as she would say of other ambivalent feelings – 'not sufficiently under-pinned'. Hers was indeed a transitional generation of women's experience.

Dorothy flew for the first time to attend David's marriage to Georgette Zackey in Woodstock, Vermont, in the United States in September 1979. Despite Dorothy's concern at the break-up of David's first marriage, she liked Georgette and they became close friends in the time she spent with Georgette prior to the marriage. Georgette was over here in a new country and Dorothy readily empathised with how strange that felt. Georgette says: "I have fond and loving memories of your mother".

At Warwick, Walter and I bought a house, which already had a granny flat at the back and this became Dorothy's for life. We added a second, and first-floor, granny flat for Walter's mother who was to be with us for eleven years and who died aged ninety-two. Neither of our mothers had any financial resources. Although they came from very different traditions, they found each other interesting and became good friends, even though they didn't understand each other's ways of cooking!

Dorothy moved up to Warwick some weeks before me because she wanted to 'keep house' for Neil and my step-son (also called Martin) who – in summer 1980 – worked hard for a fortnight at Courtaulds' Amtico plant in Coventry during the company's annual holiday. They were part of the team cleaning the machinery before the factory re-opened. Dorothy enjoyed hearing about their experiences at work. They enjoyed her thick rich stews, roasts and treacle puddings.

Walter was already living in Warwick. We had married in London in November 1979. Dorothy was present and enjoyed the day that started with all of us going to the Richmond Register Office together in a bright yellow van hired from the Local Authority's Social Services Department! It ended with us all going to see a

Dorothy tight-plaiting Naomi's hair, Easter 1979. The portrait of Martin behind was painted by his paternal Uncle Edwin Greenman, Teddington 1977

Dorothy with Neil, East Bridgford, Nottinghamshire, 1979

Dorothy's photo in her Passport, which she obtained in 1979 in order to fly to America for David's wedding. It was the first time she had flown and she arrived in the US in the tail of a cyclone that caused considerable disruption, but she regarded it as an adventure

theatre production of *The Sound of Music* following a meal in an Italian restaurant.

To the end of her life, Dorothy continued to keep a close interest in her grandchildren, writing to them when they were apart and enjoying their communications and visits. She kept some of their cards and letters. Some were long, factual and philosophical.

Dorothy became noticeably ill in early January 1981. She had spent Christmas with David and Georgette in Devon, which she much enjoyed. By the time she returned, she was already slightly unwell and quickly became seriously ill with cancer. Until the end of March, she remained optimistic, planning all sorts of things she hoped to do in the garden.

Sadly, Dorothy only had just over half-a-year in Warwick before she became ill. During that time, she made some friends and joined the local Methodist Church. The Minister, the Revd Carr, was a good friend to her. Her two-room flat was simple but elegantly furnished. From choice in her last few years, she stripped down her material possessions to bare necessities and a few treats. I am glad her teaching and College testimonials, which are printed in this book, were among the things she saved. And her manuscript, which is Part 2 of this book.

She loved her flat and also the freedom to come into the main house and join in family times, and there were many. She never intruded and knew how to respect people's need for privacy.

Dorothy enjoyed the continuity of lasting friendships, despite geographical distance and two World Wars, which altered so many facets of life. For example, every few months a childhood friend in Hythe, Lena Worthington, wrote to Dorothy and vice versa. Her last letter arrived in 1981 after Dorothy had died. Lena, who lived at Grey Halls, Albert Road, Hythe, was herself then fragile. She wrote: "Seldom a day passes without one or more of my friends coming in, and my shopping and library is all attended to. Oh! I forgot, of course you know Stanley Boulton. He and Evelyn are wonderful, visiting and helping me in many ways . . . Cooking is still enjoyable. Last week I made mincemeat and an Xmas cake. I so often have friends to tea and a nice big cake is handy."

Dorothy made friends for life wherever she went, including friends from Ipplepen, and several from the years at the Methodist Home in Chilwell. They exchanged letters and occasionally managed to meet up. Letters from Dorothy's friends after she died offer confirmation of her gifts. Here are just a few examples:

"She used to call for me to go for a stroll on Orleigh Common after tea as we both enjoyed the countryside so much" (Maud Rowe).

"I enjoyed her friendship and the things we did together while she was here. I missed her. But she was so happy in her new home and to be with you" (Ena Roberts).

"Your mother had an outstanding personality – so alive in mind and body and so thoughtful and kind to everybody. I shall never forget her kindness to me when I was ill . . . I never associated 'age' with her. To me she was always young!" (Amy Bramhall).

"She was Vice-President of the Women's Fellowship of Chilwell Road Methodist Church, Beeston. With her love and grace in leading meetings, we shall always remember her with deepest affection" (Frances Guy).

And a younger neighbour Dorothy knew for only a few months in Warwick wrote: "She was a very gracious lady who helped me over my loneliness and loss of my mother shortly after we moved. Our little chats over morning coffees were both entertaining and most rewarding" (Kristeen).

We nursed Dorothy at home until – for pain relief – she was in Warwick Hospital (the local Hospice was not yet open) for nearly two weeks at the end. Her grandchildren visited whenever they

254

Naomi lighting candles on her 20th Birthday cake as Dorothy watches, Teddington 1980

After David's wedding to Georgette Zackey at Woodstock, Vermont, USA, 1979. Left to right: Gareth (David's son), Dorothy, David, Georgette, Alyss (David's daughter) and her husband, Anthony D'Anna

Dorothy's 80th birthday, Teddington 1980. Left to right: Neil, Naomi (just!), Dorothy, me, Georgette and David

could. Neil was working in his gap year and managed to come home most weekends to share caring for her.

Alyss made a sun face to put on Dorothy's hospital locker as her granny's symbol of life.

Once, when surrounded by family – including step-granddaughter Ruth [later Ru-tee] – around her hospital bed a few days before she died, Dorothy hauled herself up on her elbows with a big effort. Then she said: "All my life . . ." and we all leaned forward expecting some wise pronouncement. She continued: "I wish I'd had curly hair like Walter!" Then she chuckled and so did we.

She was sad that David managed to visit her only once whilst she was very ill. Her illness coincided with his firm's extensive 21st birthday celebrations.

Dorothy died in the morning of April 18th 1981. Some days earlier she told me she thought she would die before Easter. It was the day before. She knew when there was no longer any common sense in trying to prolong life. And when it was wise to face death as a friend rather than an enemy to struggle against.

Walter and I were with Dorothy. She was the first loved one I was with when they died. Without my realising it, she had over the years taught me about the needs of the dying. It was a peaceful end.

Around the family, to this day, are many examples of some of Dorothy's skills, including tapestries; hand-knitted jumpers, tops[1] and waistcoats; stitch-woven and knitted bedspreads; and embroidery: but, most important, are the memories.

My sons[2] remember with affection the many holidays that we spent with Dorothy and Gilbert in Devon during their growing-up years. Gilbert usually stayed quietly at home while Dorothy would scoop us up, plus picnics, for visits to the beach or Haldon hills and sometimes to interesting places like Dartington Hall or Exeter. And, of course, luscious cakes at Madge Mellors's in Newton Abbot! Sometimes, their cousins Alison [later Alyss] and Gareth would join us.

After her death, I found my mother's Marriage Certificate. Under the heading 'Rank or Profession', Gilbert was stated to be an Author. Dorothy has a line drawn through her space under this heading. Thus, her profession as a teacher was again ignored. For posterity, on the certificate she was a 28-year-old spinster and daughter of Robert Dann. However, she wrote the story of her life before marriage, which fills in the facts as we have seen in Part 2.

Walter and I were asked if we minded Dorothy not having a Post Mortem because of staff shortages at Warwick Hospital over the Easter holiday. She would have been delighted to thus evade the system! I was glad she had moved to Teddington before moving with us to Warwick. She much enjoyed those good months with the family. It is never wise to delay what love needs to do. Dorothy never did.

---

[1] Two tunics are in Nottingham's former Textile Museum collection together with Paton's Fashion Knit books for 1974 and 1977, which include the relevant knitting patterns.

[2] Sadly, my daughter Naomi died of cancer in 1996. She and Dorothy were very good friends. When I received the photo of Dorothy from the Southlands College Archives that appears on the front cover of this book, it was a painful pleasure. Dorothy looks very much like her granddaughter Naomi in pensive mood when a young woman.

Dorothy inspecting a tall sunflower growing in our still-to-be-sorted garden at Warwick, 1980. Nearby are trunks from some of the Leylandii trees we had to remove

Dorothy (left) sitting in the garden with me, Ru-tee (my step-daughter) and a friend in the still-to-be-sorted garden that, for once, was not Dorothy's responsibility.

OTHER TITLES IN THE
'ORDINARY' LIVES SERIES

- ***Bill of Bulwell*** by Bill Cross. ISBN 0951696017. £9.95. Autobiography of a Nottingham miner born in 1918. Already a must for social history students. 2nd Edition [1998].The Lord Mayor of Nottingham gave Bill and his wife, Joan, a Civic Reception on the occasion of the 2nd Edition launch which coincided with Bill's 80th birthday. 208 pp including photos.

- ***Alice from Tooting*** [1997] by Alice Mullen (1879-1977). ISBN 0951696041. £8.95. Few working-class women of Alice's generation wrote their life story. Hers was found in a hard-backed notebook after her death. The book is 'biography, local history, social history and a lot more' *Journal of Kent History*. 208 pp including photos. Edited by Anne Bott.

- ***Flo: Child Migrant from Liverpool*** [1998] by Flo Hickson. ISBN 0951696033. £9.95 (UK). First published autobiography of a female 'child migrant'. Flo, aged seven in 1928, was sent involuntarily - like thousands of children from Britain to Australia - to add to 'good white stock', even though she had relatives willing to care for her in Liverpool. Reviews in major Australian Press, including the *Canberra Times*: 'We all know about the Dunera boys but we need to learn more about the Flo Hicksons.' 224 pp including photos. Edited by Anne Bott.

- ***Geoff: 44 years a railwayman*** [2000] by L Geoffrey Raynor. ISBN 0951696068. £9.95. Starting as a Messenger Boy at Nottingham Victoria Station in 1939, Geoff rose to be Signalman, Controller and Senior Accident Clerk. His railway life is told in the context of the rest of his life, including his wife's thirty-three year struggle with cancer. 208 pp including photos, maps and details from BR Rule Books. Edited by Anne Bott.

- **_Vic: from Lambeth to Lambourn_** [2001] by Victor Cox. ISBN 0951696084. £11.95. Vic's pre-1920 childhood in Lambeth, London, gives a rich insight into the time. Vic started work at 14 and worked as a waiter at the Waldorf Hotel, in London's Aldwych, haunt of the rich and famous. 304 pp including photos. Edited by Anne Bott.

This Series has four broad, but overlapping, readership groups:

- elders who like life stories about 'ordinary' people with whom they can identify directly or vicariously

- students and social historians looking for first-hand accounts and reliable detail

- those interested in place-specific events and people

- a growing readership who love this Series simply 'because they do'! They sometimes write and say why they like the books' content (including the photos), their friendly feel and clear print. They welcome the 'Ordinary' Lives Series as an antidote to the commercial world's obsession with celebrity.

J M, Streatham, London, writes: _"Just a note to let you know how much my husband and I have enjoyed the books in your 'Ordinary' Lives Series. We have found them interesting, educational and, at times, sad. We look forward to your next publication"_

DT, Berkshire writes: _" I can relate to this series very well."_ He is one of an increasing number of readers who collect this series.

"I found Flo: Child Migrant from Liverpool useful for a school project. I didn't know about things like this before: I mean children having to leave this country." SY, Lancashire.

For more details see www.plowrightpress.co.uk

A PROJECT OPEN TO ANY ELDER LIVING IN THE UK NOW OR AT ANY TIME IN THEIR LIFE

RUTH'S ARCHIVE gathers first-hand accounts of individual lives. Unless people take the trouble to place their experiences 'on the record', much valuable social history is lost. Often, the most important aspects of social history come to life through the detail of 'Ordinary' Lives.

To help you write your story, RUTH'S ARCHIVE has devised a special fill-in book. It offers some structure to help you to write your life story. The fill-in book can be completed in any way you choose. There is no 'correct' way! The book offers space to describe early life, work (paid or unpaid) and, importantly, participation in extended family and/or with friends, hobbies/interests, community life and much more.

This is a way of placing 'on the record' the things that YOU feel have been and are important in your life. The ARCHIVE of completed books will become publicly accessible at no charge from 2009. The fill-in books on archive quality paper are £6.00 post free from RUTH'S ARCHIVE, PO Box 66, Warwick CV34 4XE. Further details on request.

Some people take six months or more to fill in 'their' book. One woman completed the task – with much detail - in one day! So far, participants include people who have had a wide range of careers and jobs and those who have not. Every life is valuable.

"When I made myself settle down to fill this in," said one woman in her high 80s, *"I remembered many things I'd been involved with or done over the years. It makes me feel I've achieved more than I thought."*

"For many years, my activities outside work have been to do with my large family, including sixteen grandchildren, who mostly live nearby," AG.

Ruth I Johns's latest book is _St Ann's Nottingham: inner-city voices_, with 566 pages including over 1,000 photographs [ISBN 0951696092]. £19.99.

"First, it [the book] is a piece of history and the author has used the techniques of oral history most effectively to detail the social development of an inner-city over the period of the last century. But then she has gone on to analyse and suggest remedies for the problems that have arisen in that time.

"It certainly ought to ring some bells with policy makers at both local and national level." Roger Moore, University of Nottingham, in _East Midland Historian_.